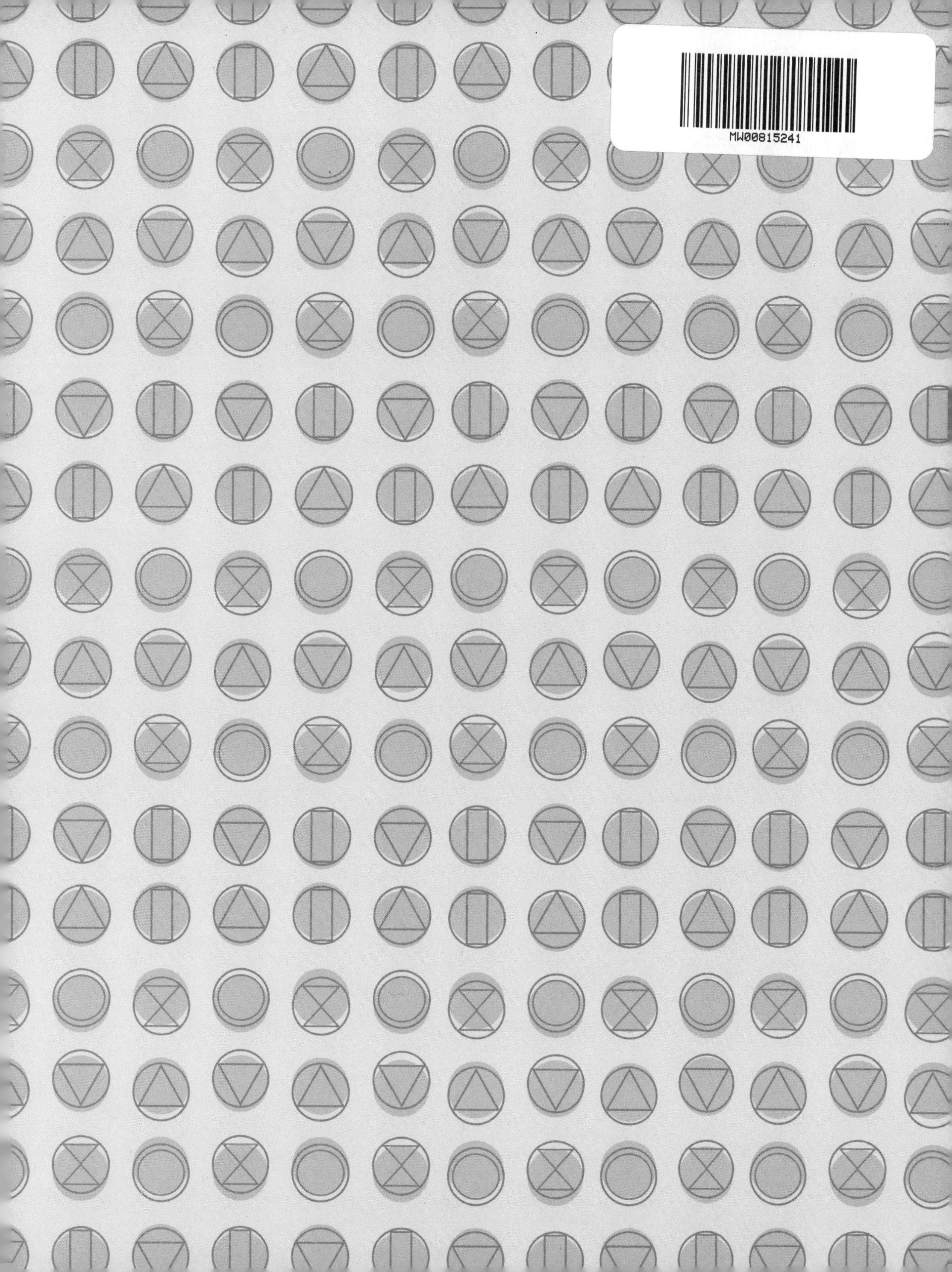

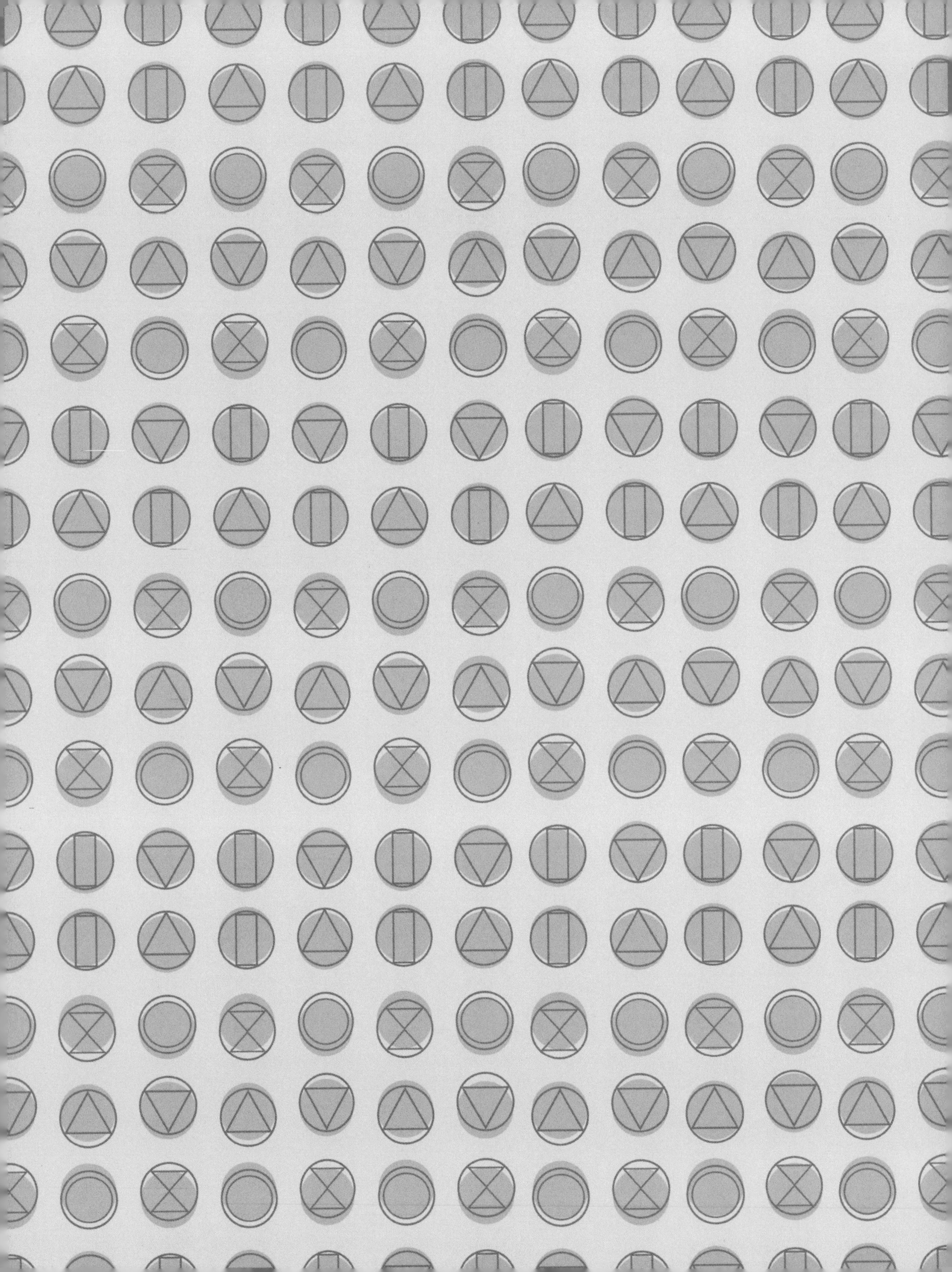

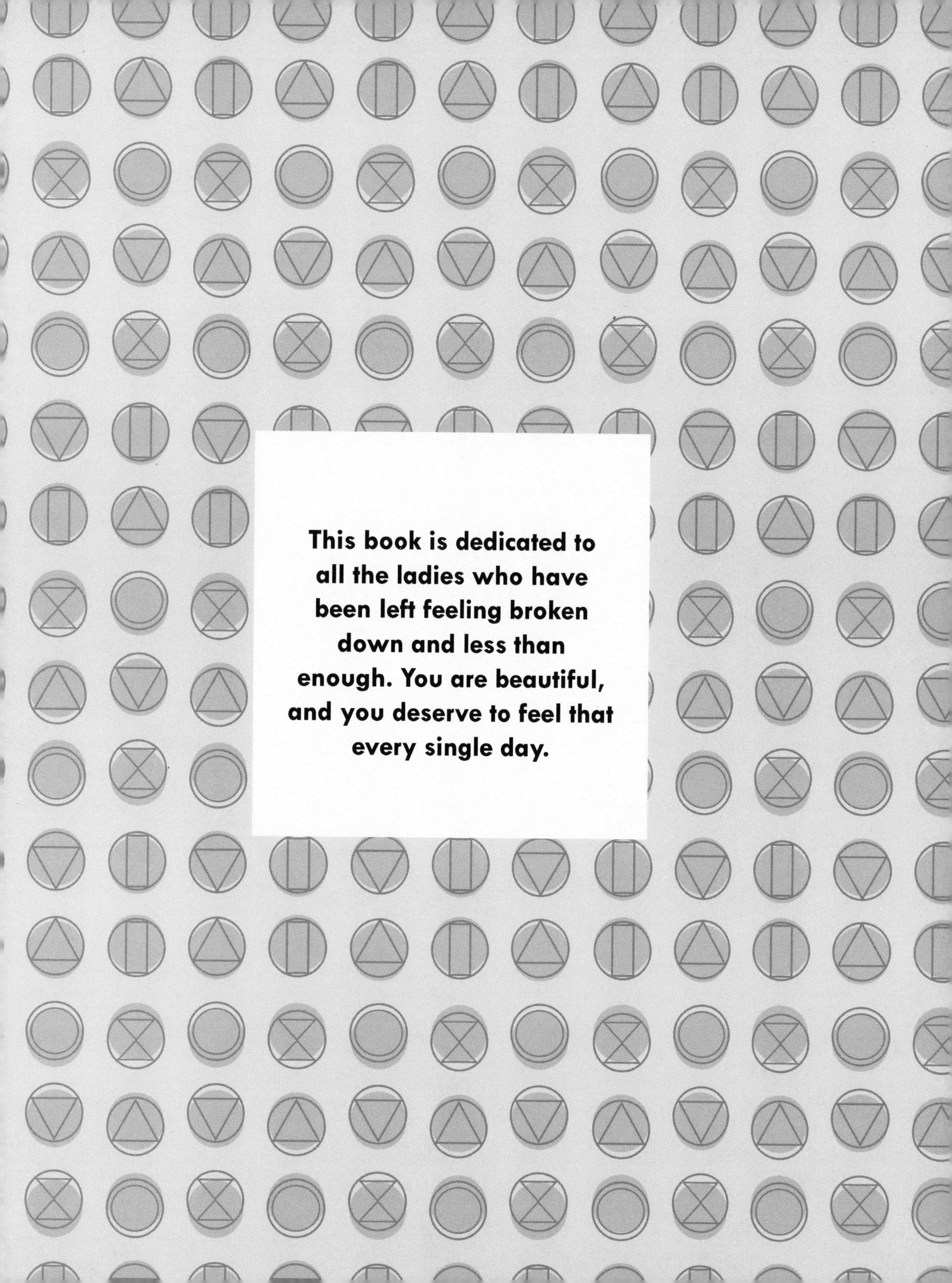

This book is dedicated to all the ladies who have been left feeling broken down and less than enough. You are beautiful, and you deserve to feel that every single day.

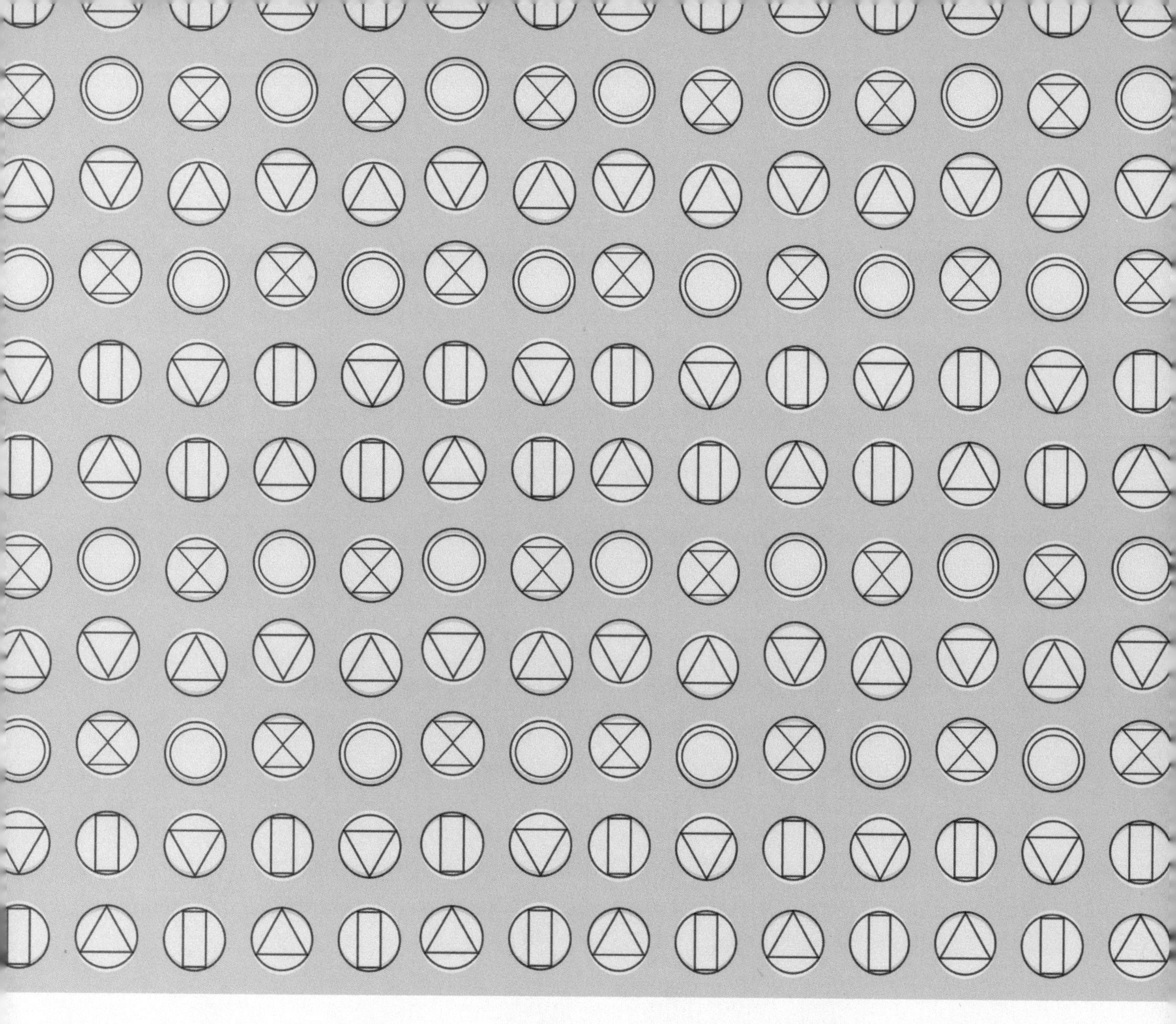

•••

WHAT PEOPLE ARE SAYING ABOUT *The Confident Closet*

•••

Testimonials

My biggest takeaway from **The Confident Closet** that I've gone on to share with everyone who will listen was what Melanie said about it not being your body's fault for not fitting into clothes "right" instead it's about tailoring and not caring about the size as much. How I felt about what Melanie said was what made a WORLD of difference for me. It was almost as if in that instant I stopped blaming myself for not fitting right but instead gave myself permission to have things tailored or simply give them the boot from my closet if they just weren't making me feel awesome - GAME CHANGER.

- BAILEY
Point Pleasant, NJ

I was shocked this week to discover that yes, I actually have a personal style! The guidelines and "homework" were so helpful to me, I realized that the things I was pinning and gravitating toward were so similar to things I wear that make me feel the most confident. I totally had an aha! moment of, "Wait, why am I buying other things and not honoring my own style?" It felt so great to realize that!

- JOY
San Francisco, CA

The Confident Closet was really helpful and I think in ways I really didn't expect it to be! The most helpful part for me was identifying what you wear that makes you feel good and focusing on those things instead of trying to make items that don't fit well or make you feel good work because you have them or they were cheap. I really thought I would focus more on organization and style but at the end of the day, it's about how you feel when you get dressed. That's something that will stick with me forever!

- KATRINA
Williston, VT

Not only has this inspired me, but I can see how it is inspiring the people around me. They are taking notice (in a good way, and yes, I'm still working on reminding myself, that it's ok for them to notice a change, and that it's not a bad thing)! I see my husband organizing and purging his things (and even talking about needing new clothes?!?!?... FINALLY....) But also in my Mom... I convinced her to get an item tailored that she loved but never wore. She looked amazing! Thank you Melanie for truly changing my life!!

- RACHEL
Dublin, CA

The biggest impact The Confident Closet had on me was helping me realize some of the habits I developed that made getting dressed a chore. Rather than feeling overwhelmed by my closet, I now feel like it reflects my personal style, getting dressed is fun again!

- JAN
Atlanta, GA

These days my closet is far more organized and clean. I have been using a lot more of my clothing and been MUCH better at purchasing items that fill in holes in my wardrobe. **The Confident Closet** was a huge help in identifying items that I will use and enjoy wearing in multiple ways, instead of just buying "fast fashion" clothes. I didn't realize how many basics I was lacking and how easy and enjoyable building a wardrobe around those items would be.

- CHRISTINE
Long Island, NY

Table of Contents

WEEK 4- YOU GOT THIS GIRL

WEEK 5 - ORGANIZE, ORGANIZE, ORGANIZE

WEEK 6 - SHOPPING & MAINTAINING

I've gotta be honest,

I'm pretty jealous of you right now.You're about to feel like you've lifted a thousand pound weight off your shoulders. You are about to wake up every morning and have a LIFE CHANGING closet. That's right. It's life changing. I truly believe that when you feel overwhelmed and frustrated about your closet it seeps into every other part of your life - from how you present yourself at your job, to how long it takes you to get ready in the morning, to how you act on a first date. That is why my mission is to help you take the steps necessary to create a closet and wardrobe you love and that works for your lifestyle.

There are two different kinds of results that exist after implementing the steps in this book. There are the results you are going to see and the results you are going to FEEL. When you are finished with this book you will have a clean closet, a clearer vision on your personal style, an organized space, knowledge on beauty practices that may have intimidated you before and so much more. All of those things lead to the other kind of result which isn't tangible but just as important. When you find clarity around what pieces to keep, and what to get rid off there is a sense of ease, knowing that what's in your closet is truly YOU. While the end result is most likely what you had in mind when you bought this book, I believe it's more important to focus on the feeling at the end of the process. That is what is going to provide the absolute best motivation as we head on this journey. While results are fantastic and a critical part of the process, when you open a well-organized closet full of clothes you love, that feeling of ease, accomplishment, and pride is truly what will get you through when you reach a challenging moment!

The Confident Closet came about from something I noticed when I first began working with women. They all seemed to have one thing in common - they wanted to FEEL amazing in their clothes. (Yup... still talking about that magic feeling.) This manifests itself in very different ways for everyone, but the sentiment is the same. Some women only feel beautiful

in clothes that are silky and soft while others are very concerned with fit, fabrication, and quality of fabrics. There are also women who play with shape and size and want to feel like their clothes are cool and trendy. All these women want to feel confident, and I guarantee you that the their versions of that are different. Which brings me to a little story.

As a costume designer in New York City, bridal stylist in Connecticut, and a personal stylist in San Francisco, one thing has always been true: I love using my style as a way to express myself. I combined my knowledge from my formal training with the influence of my surroundings and ended up finding a style I loved that was authentically me. This took an abrupt and unexpected turn once I became a mom. I needed quick, easy solutions to feeling amazing in a different body with a different lifestyle, and I had to really start applying my confidence principles in a new way. I knew when I felt like the best version of myself because I was no longer worried who would see me in the park, or at music class with my baby. Even though my body was in transition, I needed to find a way to make my clothes feel like me, fit me at different sizes, and not break the bank. It was time to practice what I was preaching and start thinking creatively.

For the first time, I was SCARED to clean out my closet. I was holding onto things that didn't fit me because of sentimental value.I wasn't taking care of my skin, hair or nails the way I knew I should to feel like the best version of myself. I no longer felt like my clothes represented the new version of me. All my clothes belonged to someone who didn't exist.

This is what I was facing every morning when I opened my closet. Umm, can you say, "TOTAL BUMMER!" So I decided to make cleaning out my closet FUN and to enjoy the process. I made snacks, put on my favorite tunes, texted my friends pics of me in my clothes, spent some time on Pinterest and really took my time. With this shift in thinking, something amazing happened, and I went through a huge, unexpected transformation.

I was not expecting the feeling of freedom that came along with purging my closet - —but it was a very real and very powerful feeling indeed. That is how The Confident Closet was born, and I couldn't be happier to share everything I've learned with you. There is nothing like releasing clothes that aren't you. You shed the old version of yourself and allow yourself to just BE YOU.

Whether you're a bride, an actress, an entrepreneur, a mom, or something in between, we all want to be able to go into our closet, know exactly where things are, and create beautiful outfits. Women want to feel confident from the moment they walk out the door. Whether you consider yourself a fashion maven or not, everyone puts clothes on in the morning, and everyone wants to feel good. So let's get you there, shall we?

The Confident Closet is broken down into six weeks, with each week focused on a different key part of not only cleaning out your closet but gaining confidence in your personal style. It will help you purge, organize, and build a closet that you love. I am sometimes met with a very loud response of, "SIX WEEKS! That takes SO LONG!" But trust me when I tell you, in order to do it right and not end up in the same place in a few months, it takes time and patience. Throughout the process, I'll also address how to gain self-confidence through your clothes, set the foundation for the best version of yourself, and basic style principles to help you define YOUR personal style. Beyond that, I also talk about organization, shopping, and maintaining. Maintaining is a crucial step in making sure you stick with your new habits, keep your wardrobe at a size that works for you, and that the work you do here stays with you forever. This book is chock full of important information for you to gain knowledge and break the bad cycles that lead you to feeling frustrated when you get dressed every day. Spreading the program over six weeks will allow you to take the time and do it right.

Throughout each week there will be diagrams, journaling exercises, tips, tricks, and more. Make sure you take the time on each assignment and treat this as an act of self care. It's like planning out your groceries for the week, or making sure you have your haircut scheduled. Not only is it important to not rush, but it's crucial to go at your own pace and take it seriously. I promise, you'll thank me later!

Before we get started, I want to remind you that cleaning out your closet is so much more than clothes. It's about memories, both good and bad. It's about who we think we should be versus who we really are. It's about love and acceptance. It's about releasing the old and bringing in the RIGHT now.

Clean out your closet the right way, and your whole life will have a new sense of ease. I'm so excited that you get to experience that glorious feeling of true shift and change. And on that note...

LET'S GET THIS PARTY STARTED!

WEEK ONE
The Beauty Basics

WHAT ARE YOUR BEAUTY BASICS & WHY AREN'T YOU MAKING THEM A PRIORITY?

What ARE the "Beauty Basics" after all? These are the weekly or monthly beauty practices that make you feel like the best version of yourself. Let's face it, whether we want to say it out loud or not, when we have waxed our eyebrows (or other lady parts, wink wink) or have a fresh haircut we feel like the best version of ourselves. In order to elevate your style, these practices are a great place to start. Now, this isn't about doing things you don't like or that you feel are extraneous. It's about asking yourself the question: "What makes me feel beautiful?" and going and doing that thing! This is the foundation that helps us feel wonderful BEFORE we put on clothes.

Knowledge is Confidence. This is a key principle to remember not just as you clean out your closet, but whenever you feel you need a little boost. Sometimes we aren't confident about something strictly because we don't know enough about it. For example if you like being tan, but don't love the idea of a spray tan or being exposed to the sun, maybe it's time to look into sunless tanners and do some research. I know it can be scary to enter unknown territory, but the only way to get past your uncertainties about style is to face them head on and LEARN.

STEP 1: Write down your favorite beauty practices:
For example: "I love me a good face mask."

Have writer's block? What if I were to say to you, "Go ahead and get your hair cut right now!" What would you say to me? Would you say, "Hell yea!" Or would you say "I don't have the time." Allow whatever comes into your head to flow onto the page like you are a 14-year-old girl who just had her first kiss.

STEP 2: Ask yourself, "Why don't I do these practices as often as I should?" This is a journaling exercise. I encourage you to write whatever comes to mind. This section is about being honest with yourself. Don't worry about solutions until later, girl!

STEP 3: Now it's time to problem solve baby! Take a look at everything you wrote and write down a possible solution for each problem or road block you have in your way. Hold yourself accountable by actively writing down how you are going to solve the problem!

The Confidence Meter

BEEP, BEEP, BEEP!

I can hear your confidence growing and growing!
The Confidence Meter is a way to measure your confidence about a beauty practice or outfit. If you are feeling really amazing about how you look and your style, that confidence meter reads at a TEN. When you are self conscious or wearing clothes that you don't like, your confidence meter will hover around a two.

The goal is to get you feeling like the 10 you are!

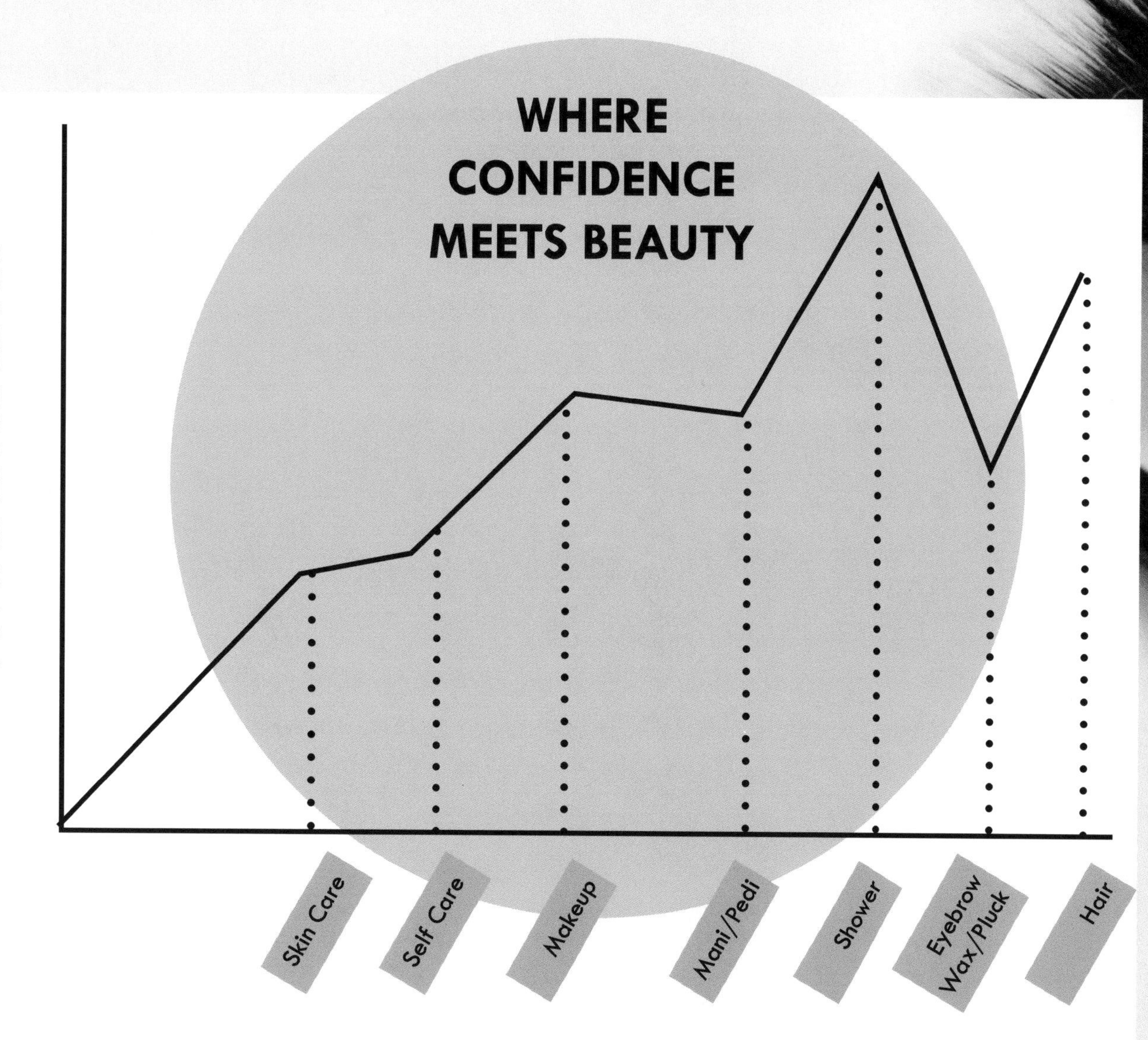
WHERE
CONFIDENCE
MEETS BEAUTY
Skin Care
Self Care
Makeup
Mani/Pedi
Shower
Eyebrow
Wax/Pluck
Hair
BEAUTY BASICS

CONFIDENCE LEVEL

MAKEUP SHELF LIFE

Makeup is one of those things we hold onto for quite a long time. The funny thing is, we usually don't wear all of the makeup we own. Your makeup actually does have an expiration date, and for good reason. I worked with professional makeup and hair artist Melissa Hoffmann to make sure you know what to keep and when to toss your makeup. By taking the time to purge your old makeup, you'll be able to not only see what you use and what needs to be replenished, but you'll also it'll also help you find what you DO have more easily. Being able to see it all means you'll use it more frequently, making for a much more efficient makeup routine.

BRUSH CARE

Clean after each use with mild detergent or a brush cleaner. You can wipe them on a cloth after each use and then do a deep clean every few months to keep them in tip-top shape.

SPONGE CARE

If it's a disposable one, toss it out after every use (or every other). If it's a high quality sponge (like my favorite the beauty blender) you can use for up to three three months as long as you clean it well.

LIQUID FOUNDATION

Water-based	Oil-based
6-12	18
MONTHS	MONTHS

* Keep two different foundations. One for when you are tanner (like in the summer or after a trip) and one for those paler winter months.

LIQUID CONCEALER
CREAM/GEL CLEANSER
LIPSTICK
NAILPOLISH

1

YEAR

POWDER/STICK CONCEALER

2

YEARS

You'll know it's gone bad because the color shifts and it starts to cause pimples.

LIP LINER

3

YEARS

EYE SHADOW

3

MONTHS

Your eyes can get irritated if you use an eye shadow that's expired!

MASCARA

2-3

MONTHS

If you pump the wand in and out you are more likely to dry it out faster.
So resist the temptation!

*Mascara can breed bacteria the more it's exposed to the outside elements. It will smell like gasoline when it's done, but you don't need to wait for the smell to throw it in the trash!

PENCIL EYE LINER

3

MONTHS

Because they are going near a mucus membrane they are more susceptible to bacteria.
You don't want to mess with it.

Showing Good Face

Things Every Woman Should Know About Taking Care Of Her Skin

Let me start by saying: I am **NOT** a skin-care expert or an esthetician; so if you have problematic skin, please speak to a professional. That being said, I am a firm believer that knowledge is confidence! There are some basic skin care facts that I'm going to share with you here that I believe can truly shed some light. In the true spirit of The Beauty Basics, if skin is your "thing," take the time to figure out what is going to work for you. Is your goal to get facials four times a year? Is it to spend a little more money on high quality products? Do what you need to do to make you feel great about your skin. I know this can be easier said than done. Skin can be **TRICKY** to figure out. I get it. But taking the time to work on it will definitely be the first step. Below are things that every woman should know about taking care of her skin. Take these facts and **RUN WITH THEM, GIRL**!

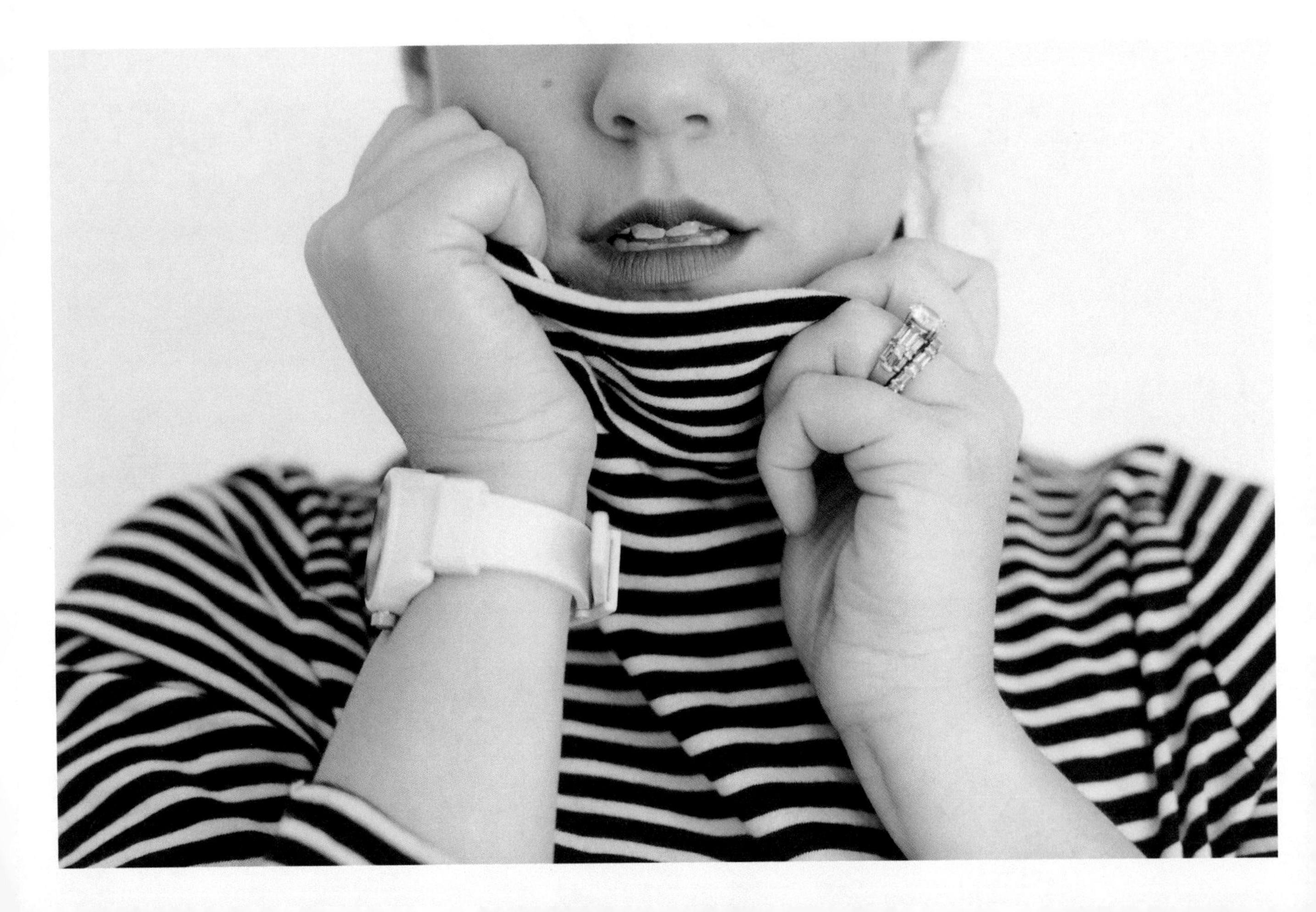

CORRECT APPLICATION OF CLEANSER:
When you wash your face, do you gently massage your face with upward circular motions? This is the best way to remove dirt and stimulate circulation.

DOUBLE CLEANSE:
The first cleanse removes surface impurities but won't really get to the pores. That's what the next cleanse is for. Doing a double cleanse, twice a day helps to ensure your face is truly clean.

TONER ISN'T THE ABRASIVE PART:
Toner smells and feels strong to the skin so people tend to think it's what's being rough on your skin. Toner is an essential step after your cleanser because it helps to balance your skins PH back to normal and can add necessary moisture. Without this step you are going to have a harder time with the rest of your skin routine so don't skip it!

TAKE YOUR TIME:
We tend to rush when washing our face. We have more important things to do like lying in bed and watching Netflix. Try your best to take your time with each product. Especially in spots that are prone to wrinkles and creases.

REMOVE YOUR MAKEUP EVERY NIGHT:
I knoooooow that you don't want to but leaving your makeup on over night is not only bad for your skin but can cause breakouts and long-term damage. If this is a huge issue for you, keep makeup remover wipes by your bedside.

HYDRATION:
However much water you are drinking...drink MORE.

PROTECTION:
As much as we all say we need to protect our skin, it can be challenging to remember all the time. An easier way to make sure your skin is protected is to use a moisturizer or foundation with SPF. I also like to use a lip balm with SPF to guard myself as much as possible!

What Does Your Hair Really Need?

It's really important to be using the right products for your hair type.

It's not as easy as just curly or straight. As you probably know, everyone's hair is completely unique with distinctive issues to tackle. A lot of brands like to simplify the process by using terms like *curly hair shampoo* or *shampoo for fine hair.* While this may be a great shampoo for you, you may also need to do a little research to find what product combination really makes your hair shine (and do all that other good stuff you want your hair to do).

First, I want you to think of the top four characteristics of your hair. Are you addressing all aspects? For example, some people have curly hair that is also very dry. Others have curly hair that is oily. These are completely different hair types and they will need different products. It goes way beyond *curly hair shampoo.* Don't be afraid to do a little trial and error here! Also, some types of hair acclimate to a product after a few months and it no longer works its magic in the same way. If this applies to you, it may be necessary to give those products a rest from time to time, and then revisit them later to see them really kick into high gear again.

Here are a few different types of hair difficulties and the products that will help solve them. When it comes to hair you have to be open-minded and patient. Your dream hair recipe is out there.

Here are some suggestions to help you find what will work for you...

FINE HAIR:

Try a thickening shampoo and conditioner to add some body to your hair.

DRY, OVER PROCESSED, HAIR:

Your poor hair girl. Two sure-fire cures to get your hair back to its former self?

1) A hair cut will get rid of the dead ends and revitalize your tresses.
2) An argan oil treatment will help pump some moisture back into your hair.

OILY HAIR:

Only use conditioner on the ends of your hair and make sure to rinse thoroughly. This will help prevent build up.

FRIZZY HAIR:

Tame that frizz with an anti-frizz serum. Just remember to steer clear of your roots.

Melanie's Tip: I'm a fan of styling creams for many different hair types. They tame frizz, add bounce and detangle. The trick is to make sure not to use too much! As my dad always says "A little dab will do ya!"

WAVY HAIR:

Seek out a product that focuses on enhancing the wave and not weighing it down. Sea salt spray also adds a nice beachy, "I woke up like this" feel.

CURLY, THIN HAIR:

Avoid gels. They are too crunchy and won't give your hair a natural look.

ULTRA CURLY HAIR:

Your hair needs moisture to keep those curls thriving. Try a leave-in conditioner on top of your regular conditioner for an added boost of love.

WEIGHED DOWN HAIR:

Use a clarifying shampoo once a month to remove build up.

Melanie's Tip: Instead of drying your hair with a towel, try a t-shirt. I t helps to control the curls without causing frizz.

YOU'VE GOT A PROBLEM, YO, I'LL SOLVE IT...

There are a lot of common problems and myths that come along with taking care of your skin, hair, nails and body hair. Some of these challenges can cause us to become discouraged, give up, or call it quits before you've even begun. I want to remind you how important it is to be persistent about solving these issues (to the best of your ability). If your nails are a huge source of insecurity for you because they are brittle or yellow, let's figure out how to make them something you **LOVE**. If you are scared to get waxed but you have a deep hatred for unruly hair, it's time to face your fear and **DO IT**. Below are some of the most common problems and some solutions you may not of heard before. I know that these may seem like simple solutions to difficult problems. The goal is to teach you something you may not know, and to get the wheels turning on what it is that will make you feel as fabulous as you ARE. **YOU GOT THIS**!

PEELING NAILS:

If your nails are peeling, it's probably from too much water exposure. Start to remedy the situation with wearing gloves to do dishes and limiting your exposure to hot water.

*Another reason for peeling nails could be from an iron deficient diet. Time to bulk up on spinach!

WEAK OR BRITTLE NAILS:

Make sure you are hydrating from the inside out. Drinking lots of water can do wonders for your nails! Actually, it is also wonderful for your hair and skin, drink up!

BODY BREAK OUTS:

Make sure to shower immediately after the gym. Also, wash your face before and after exercising. When your makeup mixes with sweat it causes clogged pores and breakouts instantly.

EXTRA, EXTRA DRY SKIN:

Opt for an oil instead of a face lotion. Skin oils continue to hydrate all day.

SENSITIVE & IRRITABLE SKIN:

Find products that use goat's milk since it's not as harsh on skin.

A SCAR THAT WON'T GO AWAY:

The tiniest bit of vitamin E oil can help heal scars.

BANGS THAT ARE CAUSING BREAKOUTS:

Since your bangs can cause you to sweat more on your forehead make sure you are washing your bangs daily. Even if you don't wash the rest of your hair every day, the bangs need to be cleaned.

- Focusing on the things that make you feel beautiful will add a confidence boost and give you the foundation you need to keep you feeling your best.

- It's important to go through your makeup and hair products and make sure they aren't expired.

- Knowledge is power. If something makes you feel insecure, take the time to learn more about it. The more you know, the more you can shine EVEN more.

- Confidence is a journey and a process. Be kind to yourself!

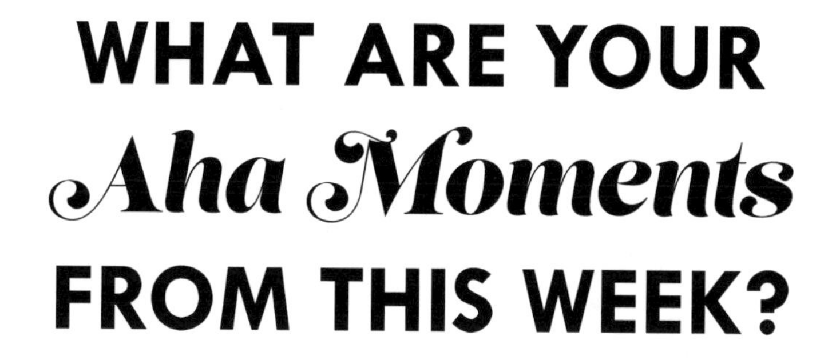

WHAT ARE YOUR *Aha Moments* FROM THIS WEEK?

What actionable steps can you take after reading **The Beauty Basics**? Write them below before you move onto Week Two!

YOU DID IT!

As a gift from me to you head to theconfidentcloset.com/bonus for an added bonus!

WEEK TWO

Personal Style, Fit, & Inspiration

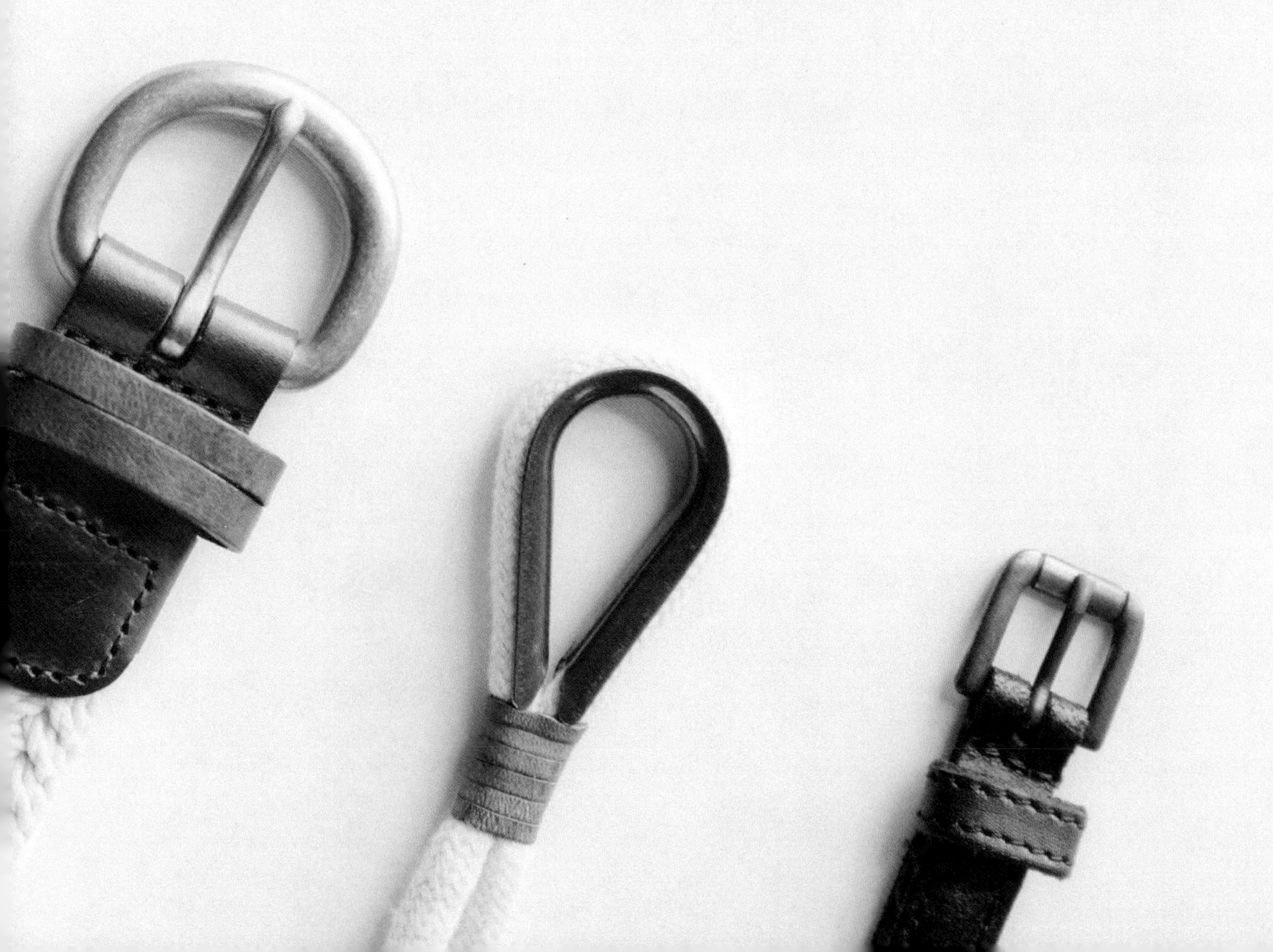

While I'm sure you are itching to get into your closet,

it's important for you to first really know your style. Otherwise, you'll end up keeping things you won't wear, or you won't be clear on what to get rid of when you are purging. This is the number one reason women aren't able to maintain a functioning wardrobe after they clean out their closets. They don't have the clarity to know what fits them correctly or what is truly their style. This leads to an endless cycle of filling their closet with the wrong things. It really just takes some time, focus, and asking the right questions. That's why I'm here.

This chapter also talks about the importance of fit. You may know your style well, but if the clothes you are wearing don't fit well, you still run the risk of feeling insecure. There are a few main culprits of an ill-fitting item. When something doesn't fit correctly it could be the wrong bra, the wrong size, or the wrong length. That's why we discuss the importance of bras and how to dress for your shape.

There is a true art to finding the balance between fit, style, and putting an outfit together; but once you understand your body and personal style, it all falls into place. This is the week to make those connections for yourself so you are ready to tackle your closet purge next week.

WHAT'S YOUR LAYERING STYLE?

The perfect pop of color

Sophisticated, chic, and warm

Where function meets fashion

Versatile, edgy, and classic

ME & MY STYLE

Identifying your style can be tricky business. It's also crucial when it comes to making decisions while shopping and outfit planning. I have found that having confidence in your personal style boils down to ***three*** things: clarity, inspiration, and conviction.

Once you have clarity, inspiration, and conviction about your style you are able to make those style decisions with more ease, and walk out the door feeling confident, self assured, and oh so stylish.

ONE Clarity :

If you don't feel like you completely know your style, this usually comes from a lack of clarity. It's not only important to be clear on what you like, but what makes you feel fabulous. In order to become very clear on your style take the time to listen to your instincts. On the next page there is a roadmap to help you on your path to a clear and unique sense of style.

TWO Inspiration:

Inspiration is one of the most crucial aspects of individual style. No matter what kind of style you have, something or someone is influencing you. Inspiration can come from anywhere. It can be literal - like seeing someone else wearing something you like - or it can be abstract, like the colors found in nature. Our lifestyle also inspires and affects us.

THREE Conviction:

Ok, so here's the deal. Finding the inspiration and clarity on your style is just the beginning. Having the confidence and conviction to rock your exclusive, fashionable style is the last piece of the puzzle. This part is easier said than done, but I know you can do it! You can't go from feeling insecure to strutting down the street in a day. Having certainty with your style takes time. But it starts with really loving what you are wearing and feeling like it's a great representation of who you are.

Personal Style Clarity Road Map

GET INSPIRED

Head to Pinterest, magazines, style books or the internet to collect inspiration.

STYLE ICONS

Whose style inspires you?

ANALYZE YOUR FAVORITE LOOK

Why do you love it?

UNDERSTAND WHAT FLATTERS YOU

But don't let it limit you!

KEEP YOUR LIFESTYLE IN MIND

Look at your day-to-day activities.

DEFINE YOUR STYLE IN 4-6 WORDS

Are you romantic, edgy, cozy, bold...?

A CLEAR VISION OF YOUR PERSONAL STYLE

INSPIRATION, CLARITY & CONVICTION:

When trying to decipher your unique style, it can sometimes be overwhelming to know where to start. Chances are you know your style better than you think you do. If you don't already have a Pinterest account, create one now. Go ahead... I'll wait.

Great! Now that you have your Pinterest account keep reading because I KNOW it's gonna be hard to get your attention after you've been introduced to such an amazing source of inspiration. Pinterest is the easiest way to collect all your fashion brilliance in one place. Once you've perused and been inspired by everything Pinterest has to offer, I want you to start to notice trends.

A. Find three trends that continue to pop up on your Pinterest boards. Do you constantly pin clothes that have stripes or outfits with layers? Those are specific, distinctive things you are attracted to. Take the time to notice them; these elements will most likely be what you are attracted to when you shop as well.

1 ______________ 2 ______________ 3 ______________

B. Identify two of your style icons. Whose style do you love AND would like your style to be similar? Of course, I don't want you to dress exactly like anyone else. Remember, this is for inspiration. That being said, sometimes it's nice to look to certain celebrities for outfit ideas and to be motivated to try something new.

1 ______________ 2 ______________

C. Pick four words that describe your style. These words can be anything that you think defines what you wear and how you like to be perceived. Words like comfy or cozy can work just as well as nautical or bohemian. Have fun with it!

1 ______________ 3 ______________

2 ______________ 4 ______________

Trusting your Intuition

CAUSE GIRL, YOU GOT THIS

When you go into your closet, do you feel 100% confident about your choices? Do you go to the store and know exactly what looks good on you? How about accessories? How do you feel when you are getting dressed every morning? Chances are if this is something that gets you down there is one MAJOR thing that's missing.

You are missing the **TRUST** in your intuition.

What would it feel like to go to your closet and expect that you have the knowledge and skill to put together an amazing outfit? I'd like to suggest you give yourself a new frame of mind. Instead of heading to your closet with dread and doubt, I'd like you to open your closet doors saying, "I got this." Instead of disbelieving your ability every step of the way, I'd like you to TRUST that your gut and instinct won't steer you in the wrong direction. No one knows YOU better than you, right? So no one else can give you the answers on what makes you feel amazing.

Of course, I understand that there is more to it than that. That's why we focus on ways to help you identify your style, find inspiration, know what flatters you and ways to pump up your outfit with accessories. But intuition is SO powerful. I'd like you to take a moment to think about what it would be like to trust yourself when it comes to your wardrobe. What would it take for you to feel confident in your abilities? Is it knowledge? Is it something deeper? WHY do you doubt your ability?

On the next page there are some journaling questions that I'd like you to take the time to answer. Really listen to yourself and write whatever comes to you instinctually. Remember, no one else will see this so you can be totally honest and real. That's the best way to get to the root of the issue and make a real change.

QUESTIONS ABOUT YOUR INTUITION IN YOUR CLOSET:

1. When you are getting dressed in the morning, what goes through your mind?

2. Where does the most stress happen when you are putting together an outfit?

3. If someone gives you a compliment on what you are wearing, what is the first thing you think of?

4. If you could paint your ideal situation when getting dressed, what would it look like?

5. Now take your answer from number four and start to trouble-shoot and problem solve.
What do you think would make this a reality for you?

The Art of Accessorizing

When it comes to accessorizing there are three kinds of people:

ONE

THE
"I DON'T KNOW HOW TO ACCESSORIZE SO I DON'T WEAR ANYTHING."
KIND OF PEOPLE

TWO

THE
"I DON'T FEEL CONFIDENT IN MY ACCESSORIZING ABILITIES, BUT I LOVE THEM, SO I ACCESSORIZE TOO MUCH."
KIND OF PEOPLE

THREE

THE
"I LOVE ACCESSORIZING, AND IT COMES NATURALLY."
KIND OF PEOPLE

My ultimate goal is to make every woman feel like an "I love accessorizing" kind of gal. In my experience, the nerves surrounding accessories are usually from a lack of knowledge.

That uneasy feeling that you are not 100% sure what you are doing is "right" leads to not trying at all.

Since most women either over-accessorize or under-accessorize, I'm separating you into two different sections. Here is how to know which group you fall into.

YOU ARE AN OVER-ACCESSORIZER IF YOU:

- [ ] Leave the house 10 pounds heavier from jewelry.
- [ ] Often feel you've got too much going on in your outfit, but don't know what to do about it.
- [ ] Love accessories and wear as many as possible.
- [ ] Your idea of an ideal outfit is a hat, scarf, necklace, lots of bracelets on both arms, four rings, a dress, tights, heels, shoe clips aaaaand more.

YOU ARE AN UNDER-ACCESSORIZER IF YOU:

- [ ] Get stressed at the idea of putting together a complete outfit.
- [ ] Think if you wore a ring today it means you got "fancy."
- [ ] Don't own any hats and if you do, it's for warmth only.
- [ ] You like how it looks when you see someone else wearing layered necklaces but even the idea of trying to replicate the look gives you hives.

Over-Accessorizer

1. **THINK ABOUT HOW EACH ACCESSORY COMPLIMENTS THE OUTFIT.**
Ask yourself: "What does this accessory bring to this look?" If the answer is: "Nothing." then you know what to do... take it off!
Example: You are wearing a purple top and you threw on a gorgeous printed scarf that has some purple in it. You were going to also wear big earrings to add a new element and color to the outfit. Once you see the scarf on, you realize the earrings are taking away from the look. They aren't adding anything and the scarf has become the statement part of the look. Take the earrings off, and add a simple pair of gold studs.

2. **EVERY TIME YOU LEAVE THE HOUSE, FIRST TAKE A LOOK IN THE MIRROR AND TAKE ONE ITEM OFF.**
Choose one accessory to be the statement piece. Whether that's the hat on your head or the arm party on your wrists, choose one focal point. You can still wear other accessories but keep them small.
Example: Maybe you are rocking some gorgeous hoop earrings AND a necklace with a lot of detail. These items might be stunning on their own, but in reality they are competing, and one of them should remain your accessory focal point. Take one off and save it for tomorrow!

3. **IF YOU ARE A CLASSIC OVER-ACCESSORIZER, YOU PROBABLY HAVE A REAL LOVE FOR JEWELRY.**
By wearing LESS jewelry you actually are going to be featuring it more than if it's just one of eight bracelets.

4. **THE STATEMENT PIECE IN AN OUTFIT IS SOMETIMES THE CLOTHING.**
If you are wearing a bold dress with a big print, accessorizing too much can be overwhelming. Allow the clothes to speak for themselves in those situations.

5. **SIMPLIFY YOUR MAKEUP.**
If you end up feeling like your outfit has a lot going on, there is a possibility your makeup can be contributing. Your hair and makeup are accessories too. It's important not to have heavy makeup, tons of jewelry, a bold dress and statement heels - you will end up getting lost in the mix. You are too gorgeous for that, girl!
Let YOURSELF shine.

Under-Accessorizer

1. **YOU MUST CHOOSE 3.**
Every time you get dressed, choose three "accessories" to enhance your outfit. One can be a fun scarf or a bold lipstick. Allow yourself to think outside the box!

2. **ALWAYS WEAR EARRINGS.**
Earrings instantly make an outfit feel more complete. If you start there and you forget other items, it will instantly make you look more polished.
Don't forget the other items though! I'm watching you!!!

3. **THINK ABOUT YOUR OUTFIT AS A COMPLETE ENTITY.**
It's not complete with just a top and jeans.
You need to think about what would enhance your outfit and make it feel like a "look" not just clothes. Sometimes, adding earrings, a bold lipstick, and a bracelet is all you need! You wouldn't make dinner and not season it, right? You wouldn't make dinner and not season it, right?

4. **DON'T BE AFRAID TO MIX METALS.**
A lot of time we have accessories in our jewelry collection that we like, but we don't know how to mix them. Play around! I especially like mixing metals when it comes to bangles.

5. **TRIAL AND ERROR IS YOUR FRIEND.**
Don't be afraid to try a new trend. Are you nervous to layer your necklaces? Take 10 minutes when you don't have anywhere to be and just play around. It's the best way to find out what you like. This works much better than trying to figure it out for the first time the morning of!

Ok, are you ready to cure your accessorizing-itis?!

TIME TO TAKE ACTION!

It's All About That Prep

Ever find yourself rushing out of the house and getting frustrated with how long the process of getting ready is taking in those hectic moments? In order to minimize chaos and maximize your time there is truly only one thing that helps...

PREPPING

FOUR UNIQUE WAYS TO PREP FOR THE *Best Day Ever*

Pick out your outfit the night before (Just like you did in elementary school!) This give you enough time for trying things on and helps the decision making process of accessories.

Have your go-to outfits. Knowing your favorite outfits means being able to grab and go! Make sure you take some time with your closet and pick out your top three outfits for work and play. Ain't nothing wrong with having an easy fav.

We mentioned the Beauty Basics in Week 1 of this book, but I want to say it again. Part of prepping in advance is having regularly scheduled beauty practices. Like haircuts, waxes and nail appointments. Whatever makes you feel fantastic that doesn't involve clothes!

Shower, pluck, and shave. Do whatever it takes to make you feel like a million bucks before the clothes even go on your body.

The Five Shapes of the Confident Woman

When I set out to write this book, I knew I would have to find a way to talk about different body shapes and sizes in a way that felt true to what I believe. While I do understand the need to want to learn about what is "flattering" on your body, I don't believe in talking down to yourself in the process. You'll notice when I describe each shape that I use positive self talk. I'd like you to take the time to think about how to talk about your body in a positive way.

I also want to make sure you realize that while this section talks about what is flattering to different body shapes, I don't necessarily think that it is always the number one factor when picking out your clothes. I often choose pieces that are fashion-forward and play with voluminous shape. That being said, I understand why women want to wear things that flatter, and I want to help you feel confident in all different ways.

While these are five of the most common shapes, a lot of people are a combination and it's not as black and white as one would want to believe. There are also several people who don't truly fall into any one category. So take all of this with a grain of salt, and realize it is a guideline to help you. If you feel confident in something that doesn't fit into any of these suggestions, I say, throw caution to the wind and ROCK IT. Confidence is always key!

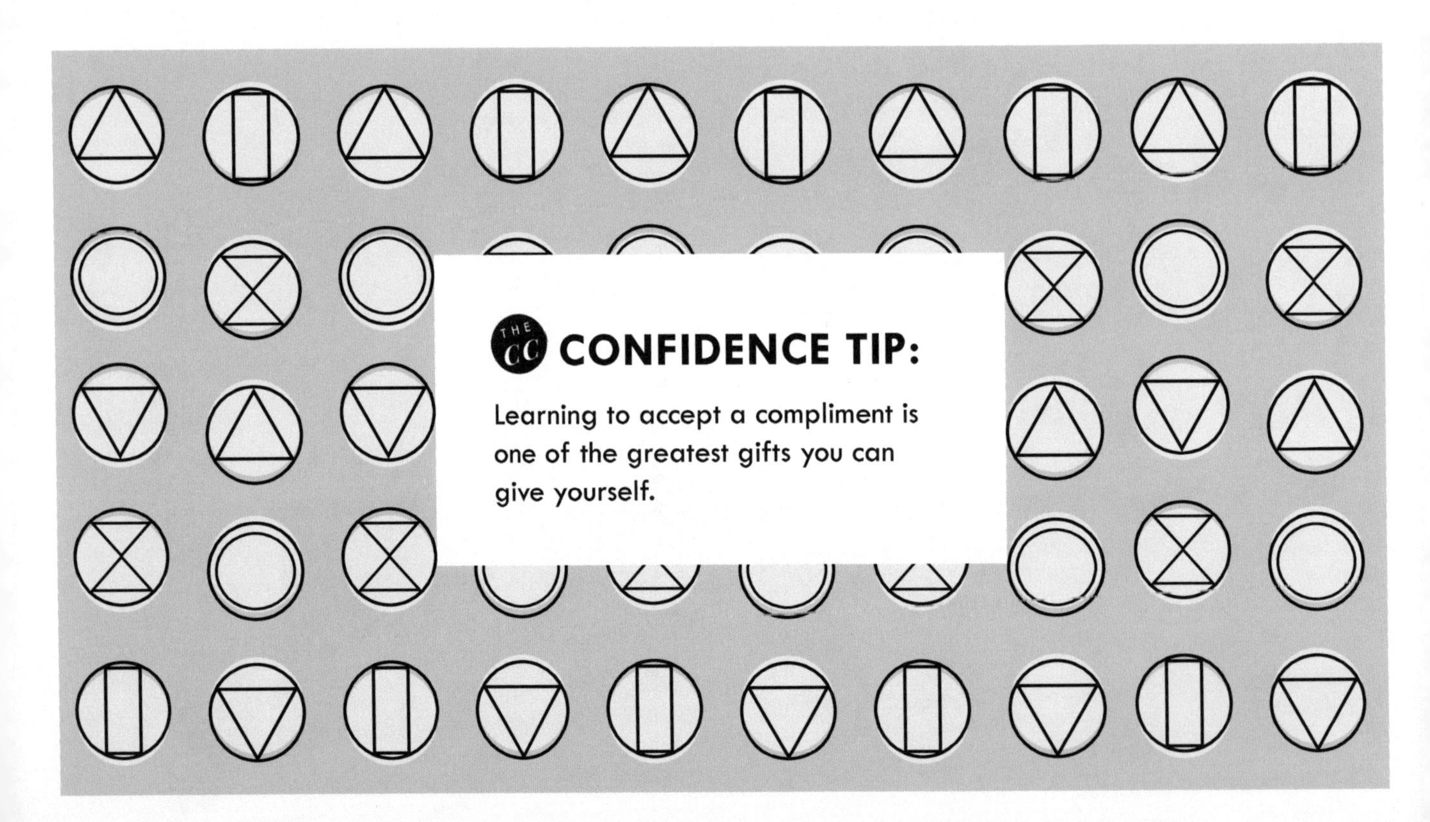

TRIANGLE

AMAZING ATTRIBUTES:

Your hips are larger than your bust and your waist gradually slopes out to the hips. You are excellent at shaking what your mama gave you. Curvaceous legs and hottie boombalottie hips. You are smaller on top creating a triangle shape.

WHAT TO WEAR:

• A fitted blazer with textural detail draws attention to the upper half of your body and creates balance.

• A detailed top centers the focus to your slim upper body and is a great way to flatter your shape.

• An a-line skirt is a great addition to your wardrobe. It features the smallest part of your waist and flares out right where you want!

• A slim boot cut or slightly flared pair of jeans helps to even out your shape and draw attention away from your hips.

• A dress with an empire waist is a great way to flatter your shape. It shows off the tiniest part of you and gives such a romantic feel.

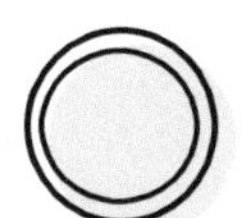

CIRCLE

AMAZING ATTRIBUTES:

You have incredible legs and a fit booty. You also tend to have an awesome bust! Your middle section makes a circle shape. You chest is on the larger side and you have rounded shoulders.

WHAT TO WEAR:

• A fitted blazer can really help to give you a great shape.

• Keep the details on your clothes at the neckline or below the waist as to not draw attention to your mid section.

• A flowy top deemphasizes your midsection. Pair it with a fitted pair of pants to show off your legs and keep the look from feeling frumpy.

• A high waisted a-line or circle skirt will help show off the tiniest part of your torso and then flair out around the midsection.

• A shift dress shows off your killer legs.

• Slim, straight, or boot cut jeans all look great on you!

• *Don't hide that gorgeous body! Circle shapes tend to want to wear flowy clothes but it ends up making them look larger.*

HOURGLASS

AMAZING ATTRIBUTES:

Damn, girl, look at those gorgeous curves! Your tiny waist is one of your favorite assets. You've got the bust and booty that everyone wants! It's just about learning how to flaunt it! Done and Done!

WHAT TO WEAR:

• A wrap dress helps to cinch your waist and accentuate those already fabulous curves.
• When in doubt, belt it. This will add definition to your waist and will always be your best friend.
• Mid rise jeans that have been tailored at the waist. Hello gorgeous!
• High waisted pencil skirts to show off your hips! This skirt may need to be altered for the best fit, but totally worth it!
• Scoop neck shirts show off your shape without giving too much away.
* No matter what, you are probably going to have to see a tailor about a few items. Having clothes that fit your shape well will make you have loads more self confidence! Make sure to go the size up and have it tailored down for the best fit.

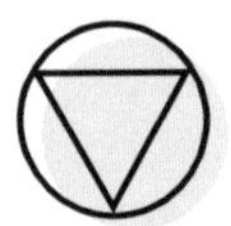

INVERTED TRIANGLE

AMAZING ATTRIBUTES:

You have a great, larger bust, bangin' legs, and a narrow waist. So many clothes look amazing on you! Lucky lady!

WHAT TO WEAR:

• Wide-leg pants help to balance your upper and lower half.
• V-neck tops help to minimize the upper body. Keep it simple. Too much volume will have the opposite effect you want.
• Drop waist dresses look so gorgeous on you.
* Keep jewelry simple on top, but go to town on your shoes. The goal is to make sure your upper half doesn't get all the attention. Even though it IS pretty stunning!

RECTANGLE (AKA RULER)

AMAZING ATTRIBUTES:

You have a gorgeous slender frame that tends to be easy to dress.
How do you manage to look sophisticated and chic all the time?

WHAT TO WEAR:

- Halter tops look great on you because of your more athletic frame.
- Shift dresses look amaze on you! Lucky lady!
- High waisted skirts or pants look great on you. They show off your fantastic shape and waist.
- A dress with ruffles or soft details will add some great softness to your shape.
- Flowy tops paired with a fitted jean is a great look for you. Stores like J Crew always have amazing blouses for women with a rectangle shape.

- Even when finding out what flatters our body, talking kindly to ourselves is everything.

- There is a balance to accessorizing that takes patience and intuition.

- Having clarity around your personal style will make it easier to make decisions when cleaning out your closet or shopping.

- Allow yourself to be influenced by your surroundings when creating your own personal style.

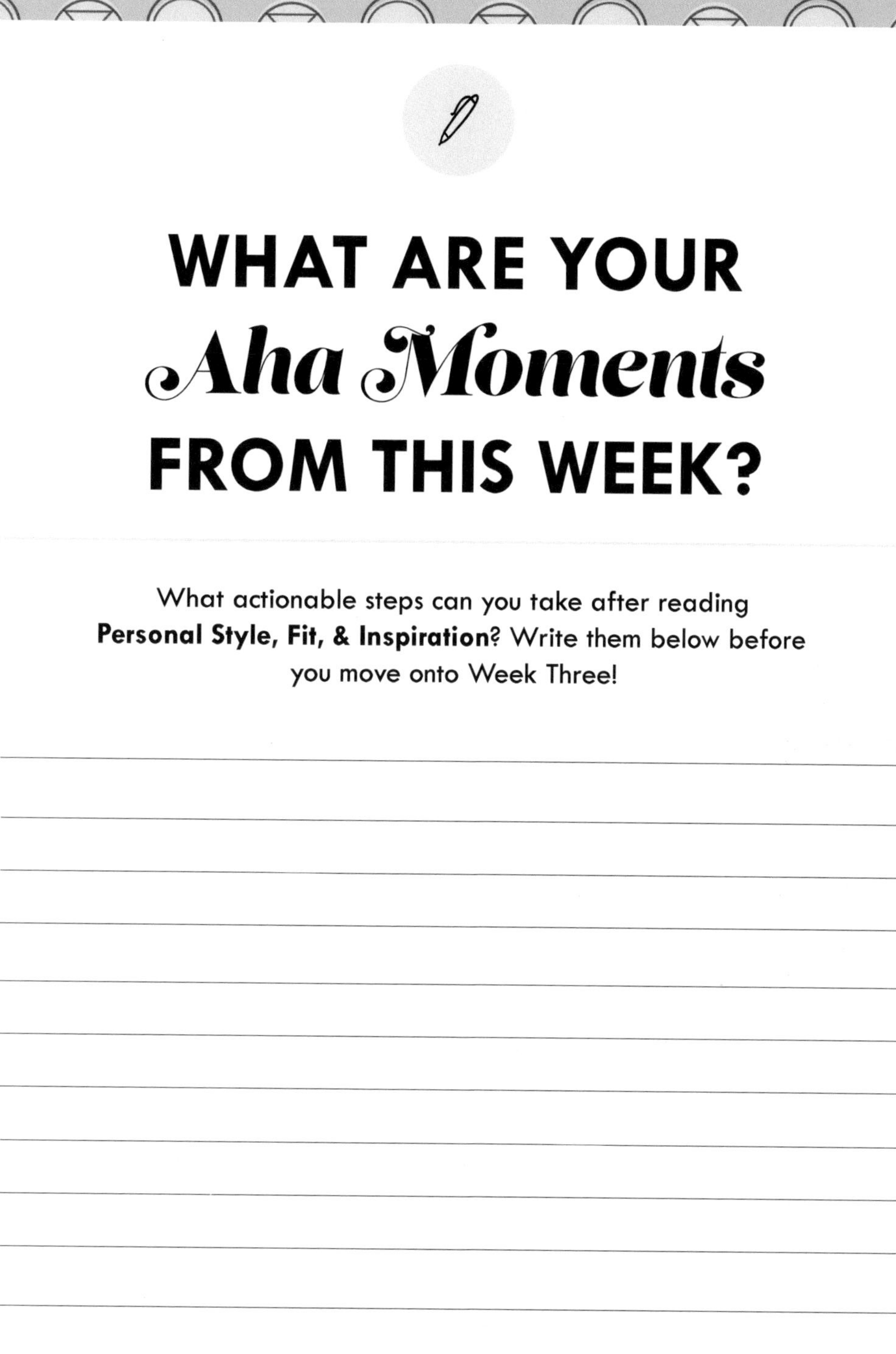

WHAT ARE YOUR *Aha Moments* FROM THIS WEEK?

What actionable steps can you take after reading **Personal Style, Fit, & Inspiration**? Write them below before you move onto Week Three!

WEEK THREE

The Big Purge

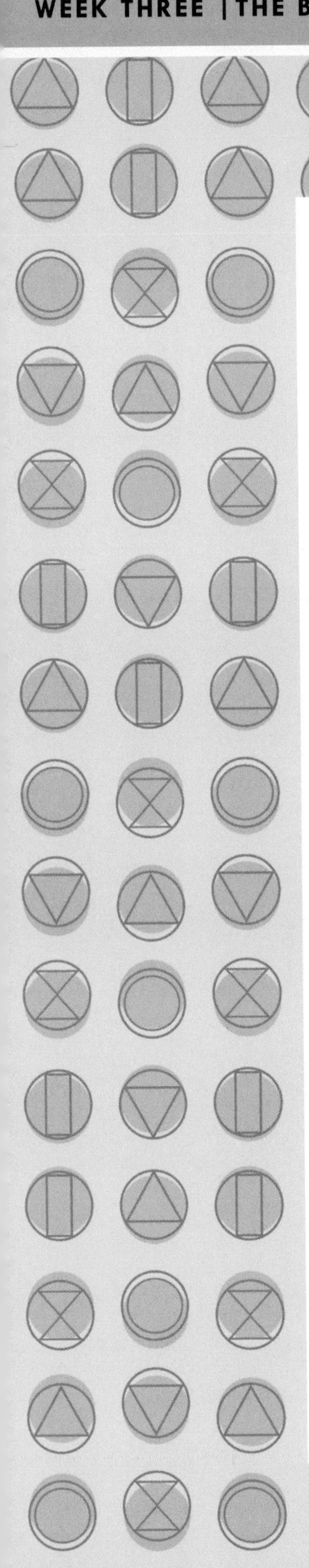

We've made it to Week 3!

The week we have all been waiting for! Before you jump on into your closet, remember to be kind to yourself. There will be, without a doubt, a moment when you are going to hit a wall. That's the point to stop, go get a snack, put on some new music and change your mindset. Don't let this break turn into watching a movie on Netflix or going out to dinner though. Too much time will bring you to a place of procrastination where things become overwhelming.

I also want to stress the importance of an organized system. Take things out in chunks and make sure when you decide to donate something it has a bag to go in that is clearly labeled. You are most likely going to be purging a lot of things and you don't want to end up confused and stressed.

Which brings me to my next point.
MAKE. THIS. FUN.
That's right! Put on some upbeat music, make yourself some snackies, and go in with a positive attitude. This doesn't need to be a chore unless you love doing chores. Just me? I digress. Let's get into that closet and get this party STARTED.

5 KEY PRINCIPLES WHEN CLEANING OUT YOUR CLOSET

1 CHUNK IT

"Chunking" is a technique that helps to reduce feeling overwhelmed. Not only do I want you to set aside a "chunk" of time, I also want you to select one area of your closet to tackle at a time. If you are having trouble deciding, start with the top left and work clockwise. It's visually appealing to your eyes and it's nice to see an instant change.

2 TAKE EVERY THING OUT

Remove everything out of the section you are working on so you can truly see it all. As you go through each item you can either place it back in the cleaned out section you are working on, or in the appropriate trash bag.

3 GO WITH YOUR GUT

As much as we sometimes think we are supposed to love it, if you know in your heart you aren't going to wear it you gotta let it go. Trust in your instinct and you'll regret nothing.

4 TRY EVERY THING ON

Hanger appeal can be a tricky, tricky beast. Sometimes we are drawn to pieces because of fabric, color, or pattern, but how does it fit on your body? Chances are if you aren't wearing it, it's due to fit and you won't know that unless you try it on.

5 BE CONFIDENT IN WHO YOU ARE NOW

Our closets are filled with pieces from different times in our lives. It's quite a mindset shift to realize it's OK to grow and change with our wardrobe. While I do believe it's important to purchase pieces for your closet that stand the test of time, it's ok to realize something USED to be your favorite but isn't anymore. It's time to let it go.

Setting the Stage

So here you are in front of your closet, ready to go... but ARE you really ready? Before you clean out your closet, you have to set the stage for the process. Take your time and have fun with it! Make sure your space feels lighthearted, fun, and is ready for you to put everything in its place as you go. Setting the stage is a game changer! Take your time so that you truly feel ready to dive deep into your closet with ease!

MULTIPLE TRASH BAGS
Note that it's important to put the items in bags and not just in a pile. Once you make the choice, you don't want your decision staring you in the face! Make labels for each bag:
a) Toss b) Donate c) Sell
d) Give to a Friend

AN OPEN SPACE
Such as a bed or a large area on the floor.

3

AN OPEN MIND
The more willing you are to letting something go, the better.

BE FRESHLY SHOWERED
Also, go do your hair! I'm serious. Go shower and then come back. You'll feel better in everything you put on!

SNACKS
This is not the kind of work that a margarita and some yummy snacks are not invited to. The more the merrier. Remember,
this can be FUN!

A CLOSE FRIEND
A friend you can text or call. Another opinion can give you a fresh take, but keep in mind that some people work better in pairs and others alone.

THIS FABULOUS BOOK & A CUTE PEN
By keeping this book with you while you purge, you'll be able to write directly inside when needed.

How to Purge Your Closet

(THE CONFIDENT CLOSET WAY)

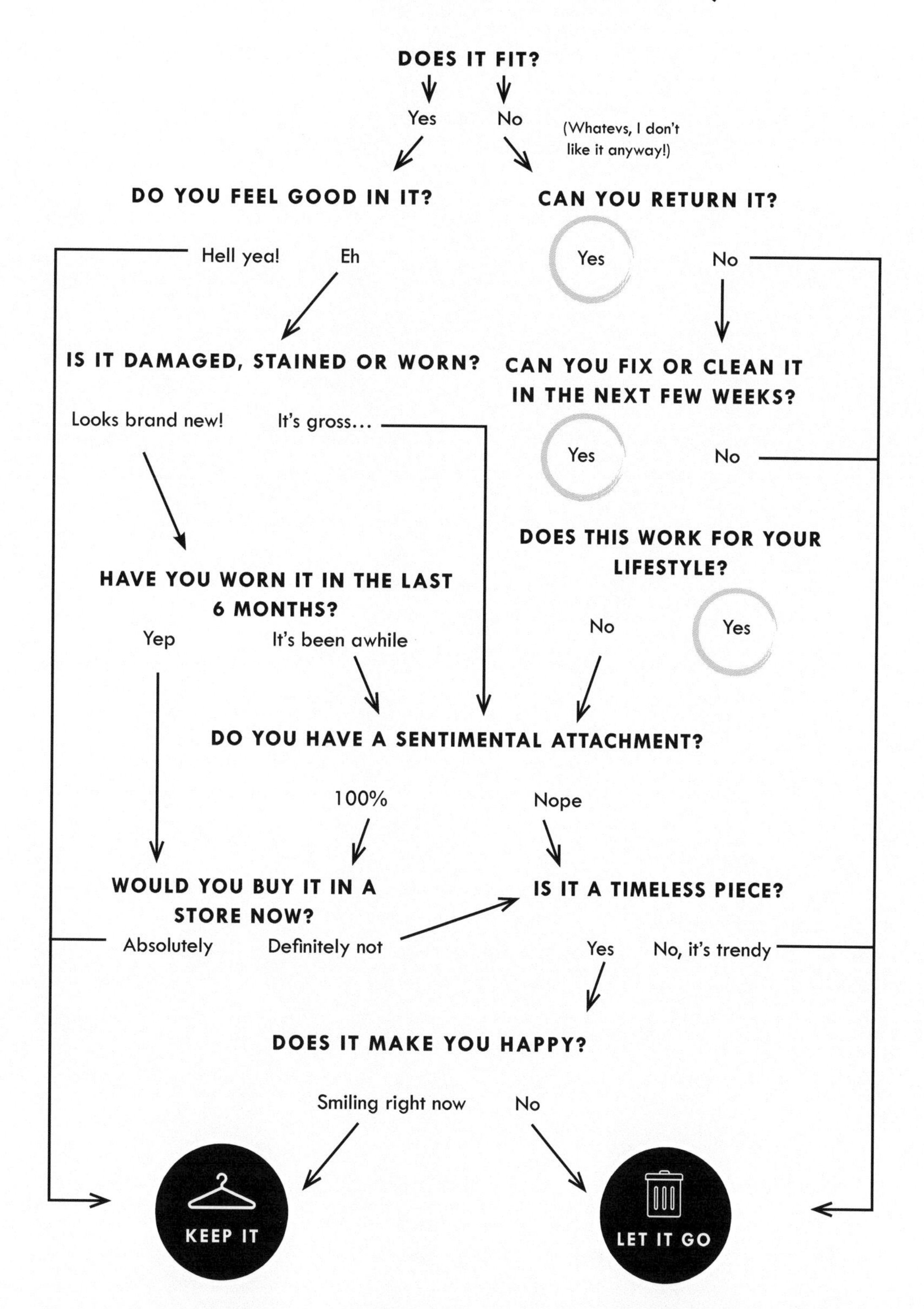

PURGING IS GOOD FOR THE SOUL (SO IS SHOPPING)

Before purging, you need to have the peace of mind that the things you are getting rid of will be replaced with something better. This is the place to do that! Make sure to write it down as you go! You will turn this into a shopping list later on, so the more specific the better!

Here is your example:

Jean Jacket - Look for one that is a darker denim. I'd like it to have a better fit and no distressing like the old one.

CONFIDENCE TIP:

Take time to get ready before going shopping for clothes. A shower goes a long way, and you'll love everything you try on so much more.

CONFIDENCE TIP:

When it comes to talking about your body, ask yourself, "Would I say this to my best friend?" If not, change your tone and remember to be kind!

Why Are You Holding On To That?

When it comes down to it, purging your closet is something you can actually do and not feel like you made a dent. This is because you aren't asking yourself the right questions about your clothes. The reason we hold on to pieces we don't wear is so deeply rooted in emotion that unless we are asking the right "WHY?" we will continue the same cycle. The list of questions on the next page is meant to cover all the bases. Sometimes you'll need to ask yourself more than one of these questions to truly crack the code. So be open minded and remember to trust your instinct.

Another way to help narrow down and prioritize is by implementing the SENTIMENTAL RULE.

SENTIMENTAL RULE - Choose five sentimental pieces. By choosing five, you end up having to choose what is more important and if you really want to keep it. You'll realize that some of the things you thought you needed actually can be donated or given to a friend. The items you keep can be put in a bin either above your closet or in a garage. They don't need to be sitting in your closet reminding you of when you were a different size, or if they aren't comfortable and you know you won't actually wear it. This is especially true when the sentimental items don't fit anymore! Who needs that staring them in the face?!

When you go to purge your closet, I'd like you to try and avoid a huge "maybe" pile. Not committing to a decision makes for more work in the long run. Instead, allow yourself no more than 10 maybe pieces. Put these pieces somewhere easily visible in your closet, and if within six months you haven't worn them, then it's time to revisit if they are truly worth keeping.

Besides your *maybe* pile and five sentimental pieces, everything else needs to be a yes or it goes into one of four garbage bags. These bags can be labeled:

TOSS

DONATE

SELL

GIVE TO A FRIEND

As you purge, answer these questions...

Yes *No*

○ ○ **Do I love it?** Not **did** I love it, but do I love it **now**. Answer this one quickly and trust your gut.

○ ○ **Do I like how it looks and fits on me?** Hanger appeal is a tricky thing. So is the mental association we make with clothes. Make sure to try everything on and then ask this question.

○ ○ **Is this appropriate for my lifestyle?** I may love wearing heels, but if I'm spending all day at the park with my toddler, it may not make sense to have 15 pairs.

○ ○ **If I were to go shopping, would I buy it now?** This one is super important. This question helps to make sure our closet is filled with clothes that feel completely like US.

○ ○ **Do I have something similar that I like more?** Sometimes we like something, but we never wear it because we have something similar we like way more. For example, if I have two black jackets, one that I *LOVE and* how I look in it, and one that is just OK but feels like it's more practical to wear (even though I don't), it becomes pretty obvious that the extra practical black jacket should go. This is a great time to give to a friend. This could become their favorite jacket!

○ ○ **Why don't I actually wear this?** This one is for reference later. By asking ourselves WHY? we are giving ourselves the opportunity to spot patterns. That way, when we go shopping we aren't setting ourselves up to create a new closet full of clothes we don't end up wearing.

○ ○ **Have I worn this in the last year?** If you haven't worn it in the last year, what makes you think you are going to start? Unless you have a good reason (i.e - you just lost weight and it now fits again) it's time to toss.

○ ○ **Is this an old trend?** While I don't really care if something is "*on trend*," there are clothes that end up feeling dated. This can also fall under the category "*Would I buy this in a store if I saw it there today?*" If it's no longer in fashion that could be the reason you aren't wearing it.

A Complete Confident Closet CHECKLIST

Here is a checklist for a concise wardrobe that includes all seasons. Of course, if you live in Southern California, you may not need as many sweaters, but you'll probably want more than one pair of sandals. Use this checklist as a guide and customize it to your lifestyle (ie. diaper bag isn't gonna be on everyone's list). Also, you may live for working out, and do it every day. In that case you may decide to up your work out gear, or you may decide working out is gross and remove that section all together. You do you, and customize this list to suit your needs.

TOPS

- ☐ Cozy high quality sweater (neutral color)
- ☐ Heavyweight sweater
- ☐ Lightweight sweater
- ☐ Quirky shirt (for your more adventurous side)
- ☐ Silky blouse
- ☐ Lightweight camisole (dressed up or down)
- ☐ Striped long sleeve t-shirt
- ☐ White cotton oxford button down
- ☐ 5 T-shirts (various colors)

PANTS

- ☐ Boyfriend (relaxed) jeans - light wash
- ☐ Skinny jeans - dark wash (i believe 95 % of people can wear skinnies...just trust me)
- ☐ 2 More jeans in your preferred fit
- ☐ Dress pants (in neutral color)
- ☐ Colored pant (jeans or pants)
- ☐ 2 Pairs of high quality leggings
- ☐ Lightweight loungewear pants
- ☐ Medium to heavyweight sweatpants
- ☐ 2 Pairs of shorts

SKIRTS & DRESSES

- ☐ Lbd (obvs)
- ☐ Shirt dress
- ☐ Maxi dress
- ☐ Summer dress
- ☐ Date night dress
- ☐ Formal dress
- ☐ Maxi skirt
- ☐ A line skirt
- ☐ Pencil skirt

OUTERWEAR

- ☐ Denim jacket
- ☐ Trench coat or rain coat
- ☐ Winter coat
- ☐ Casual jacket/blazer
- ☐ Sweatshirt
- ☐ Leather or bomber jacket
- ☐ Cardigan

SHOES

- ☐ Black pumps
- ☐ Neutral flat
- ☐ Sneaks
- ☐ Tall boots
- ☐ Short boots
- ☐ Sandals
- ☐ Rain boots
- ☐ Snow boots
- ☐ Flip flops
- ☐ Statement shoe

ACCESSORIES

- ☐ Warm scarf
- ☐ Silk scarf
- ☐ Sunnies
- ☐ Neutral skinny belt
- ☐ Wide brown leather belt
- ☐ Statement belt
- ☐ Umbrella
- ☐ Evening clutch
- ☐ Brown handbag
- ☐ Black handbag
- ☐ Winter hat
- ☐ Winter gloves

JEWELRY

- ☐ Gold or silver studs
- ☐ Pearls
- ☐ Everyday watch
- ☐ Fancier watch
- ☐ Statement earrings
- ☐ Statement necklace
- ☐ Gold long necklace
- ☐ Simple one strand necklace
- ☐ 1 Set of bangles
- ☐ 2 More assorted bracelets

ASSORTED EXTRAS

- ☐ 2-3 Bathing suits you adore
- ☐ Cute pjs
- ☐ Straw hat
- ☐ Red dress for holiday parties
- ☐ Jumper
- ☐ Gym clothes
- ☐ 4 Pair tights/stockings
- ☐ A great pair of loafers

SO WHAT HAVE WE LEARNED? Week Three

- Before you purge your closet, make sure you've set the stage and have the right mindset.

- Don't rush and remember to have fun.

- Make sure you are asking yourself the right questions as you purge, keeping nothing that you wouldn't wear right now.

- Holding onto clothes for sentimental reasons can cause more harm than good.

WHAT ARE YOUR *Aha Moments* FROM THIS WEEK?

What actionable steps can you take after reading **The Big Purge**?
Write them below before you move onto Week Four!

WEEK FOUR

You got this, Girl

Now that you've done the bulk of the purging...

this week focuses on making sure those purged clothes actually make their way out of your house. It won't feel like a complete project until they're no longer on the floor of your living room in garbage bags. Also, you don't want to be tempted to go back on some of your decisions. Once you make the decision there is NO LOOKING BACK!

For some people this week is also a grace period in case you aren't completely done cleaning out your closet. You may need to go through that section of your closet you have successfully avoided (*cough cough*...coat closet...*cough cough*) and this week gives you the opportunity to do so. Take this time to really be thorough and don't lose your momentum!

This week is also the time to do a mental check-in. How is your confidence doing after trying on all your clothes? Are you feeling excited or nervous about the fact that you now need to replace the items you purged? Allow yourself to take a minute to reevaluate where you are on the confidence meter and think of new and creative ways to boost yourself up. Maybe this means going back to the beauty basics and getting a haircut or spending some time focusing on your personal style on Pinterest. This book is designed for you to go back and revisit several times to keep you accountable and on track.

CONFIDENCE TIP:

If you can't see it,
you won't wear it.

What To Do With The Stuff You Don't Want

Sell Your Clothes:

THERE ARE SEVERAL COMPANIES ONLINE THAT MAKE IT ALMOST TOO EASY TO SELL YOUR CLOTHES. MOST OF THEM FALL INTO TWO DIFFERENT CATEGORIES:

WE'LL SELL IT FOR YOU:

ONLINE:
Some companies make it easy to sell your clothes without communicating with the seller. These companies provide a bag with a shipping label, so all you need to do is place the clothes in the bag and bring it to the post office. You make less money but you also don't do nearly as much work.

IN PERSON:
Consignment stores will either take your clothes and give you a lump sum right there, or you'll get notified when pieces are sold. These stores only take higher quality pieces so you'll usually need to bring whatever they don't want to a donation store afterwards.

YOU SELL IT YOURSELF:

Ebay, Poshmark and several other online marketplaces make it possible to sell your gently used clothes online. What may not be working for you could be someone else's new favorite piece! You make more money this way since it's direct and you set the price.

Donate to:

GOODWILL

The Goodwill has over 2,900 locations where you can donate your used clothes. When you donate, and someone buys your clothes that money goes towards job training and other services.

SALVATION ARMY

This is a church-affiliated donation center focused on helping the needy in several different ways all over the U.S.

HOMELESS SHELTERS

Local homeless shelters are always looking for clothes for the homeless especially items like coats and shoes.

CHURCHES/TEMPLES

They always have a place to donate clothes.

DRESS FOR SUCCESS

An amazing organization that provides underprivileged women clothes for interviews.

THE CINDERELLA PROJECT

A great place to donate your old prom/bridesmaid/formal dresses. There are Cinderella Projects in NY, VA and NH, but there are local projects doing similar things!

FREECYCLE.ORG

A website where you give/get stuff for free.

Other Creative Solutions:

Project Repat will turn your old t-shirts into a blanket.

Give to a Friend who will love it!

Clothing Swap Parties where friends all come together and trade the clothes they no longer want for something new. This is one of my favorite pastimes.

Have a Yard Sale and get rid of some other knick knacks around the house while you're at it!

Donate Old Eyeglasses by contacting a local vision clinic. They'll take those old spectacles off your hands...or face.

CONFIDENCE TIP:

Ever notice that the more jam-packed your closet is the more you gravitate towards the same few things? Having fewer pieces you love will help you feel like you have more options!

All about underwear...

Learning to accept a compliment is one of the greatest gifts you can give yourself.

Underwear is by far the most neglected thing for most women in their wardrobe. Since it's not seen by (the majority of) other people, it ends up being treated like your junk drawer. You know that drawer in your kitchen or office, where you just throw all your unwanted stuff? Same thing. Let's make sure your underwear drawer doesn't become that drawer too!

SEE YA LATER, ALLIGATOR

Does this underwear still fit correctly?
When cleaning out this drawer you may realize how many pairs don't fit well anymore! Underwear (especially cotton) tend to not wear extremely well. Other pairs you can have for a long time and they don't show any signs of getting older. Those are keepers.

Are there any holes, rips, or significant wear and tear?
There really doesn't need to be too much explanation here. Toss 'em!

Is this a style I still like to wear?
I used to be someone who wore a lot of thongs. I was a spritely 21 year old who really enjoyed it! I haven't worn one in YEARS unless the dress calls for it. I recently realized that even though this underwear was still in good shape, it was just taking up space in my drawer. I kept a few that were functional and got rid of the rest.

When was the last time I wore this pair of underwear?
If it hasn't been worn in a few months, PEACE OUT.

Is this pair of underwear comfortable?
Underwear can (and should) be pretty, but ultimately, it HAS to be comfortable. You won't wear it otherwise. No one likes to be messing with an uncomfortable pair of underwear in public, or worrying about when they are gonna get a chance to pick their wedgie. Am I right?!

Does this underwear serve a purpose?
Do I have outfits that I have to wear this pair of underwear for? Those specialty pairs of underwear need to stay UNLESS you don't wear the dress that needs the special underwear. Chances are if you are going to get rid of the dress, get rid of the panties too. Treat them like a pair so that you don't dump the dress and keep the totally non functioning underwear by accident.

Some days you aren't feeling as confident as you might like. Below are a few ways to help you out of that inevitable funk and back to being the fabulous and confident goddess you KNOW you truly are!

ADDING A LITTLE PEP IN YOUR STEP

(It's all about self-love and brightening your day.)

WEAR RED LIPSTICK

THROW ON A FUN PAIR OF SHOES

PUT ON LINGERIE THAT IS JUST FOR YOU

BUY YOURSELF FLOWERS

MAKE YOUR BED

WRITE YOURSELF A LOVE NOTE

Your Orchid & Your Onion

I have a daily practice that I do with my friends and family where we talk about the best and worst thing that happened in our day.

We call it **OUR ORCHID & OUR ONION.**

Your orchid is the bee's knees. It's that thing that made your day a little brighter and a little sweeter. Or in the case of *The Confident Closet*, the best thing that's happened to you since you've started the course or since you started purging.

The onion is … well … a little less sweet. In fact, it's the stinky stuff. This is the stuff that has been a little rough. It can be very cathartic to allow yourself to say "Gosh, that was hard," and then find an optimistic lens to view that hardship through.

I usually find that my orchid is super long because I have so much to say about it. My onion tends to actually not be as bad as it had originally seemed. This puts so many things in perspective for me.

Take a minute at the end of the day and acknowledge the best and worst part of the purge. This allows yourself to really be honest and gives you some perspective.
Write away! Don't hold back!

ORCHID

ONION

WHAT HAVE YOU BEEN AVOIDING?

This is the time to address your issues head on. You are about to get into organization and shopping, and you don't want to tackle that yet if you don't feel like you've done enough in your closet and with your personal style. Give yourself a reward after completing a task and you might find that extra motivation to get everything done!

WHAT DO I GET FOR NOT AVOIDING MY CLOSET?

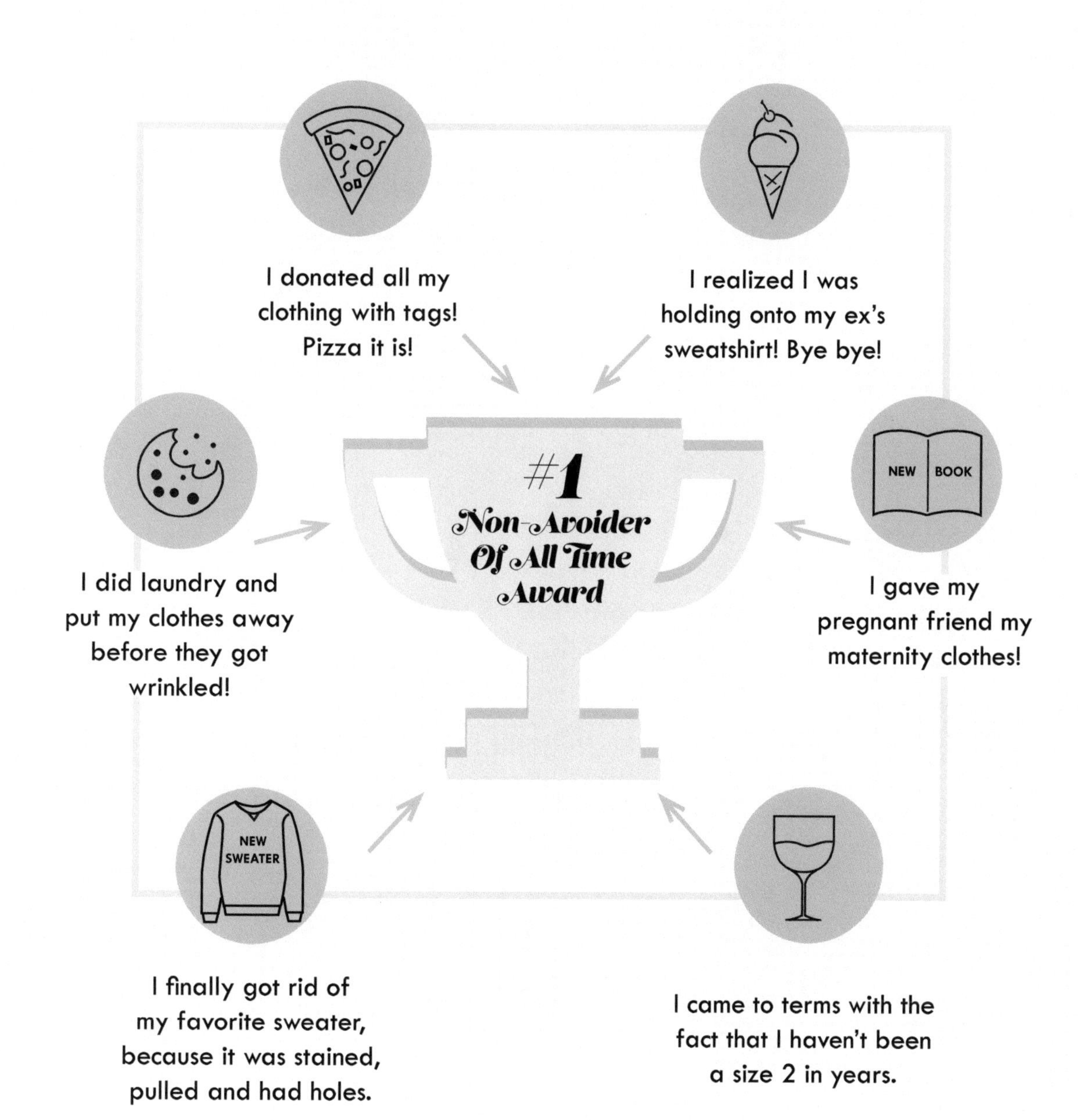

SO WHAT HAVE WE LEARNED?

Week Four

- Once you've purged it's important to get rid of your clothes or the job won't feel done.

- Remember to clean out hidden spots, places you've been avoiding, and any other closet you've been forgetting about.

- No. More. Avoiding.

- It's much more rewarding to give your clothes a new home than holding on to them to collect dust in yours.

WHAT ARE YOUR *Aha Moments* FROM THIS WEEK?

What actionable steps can you take after reading **You Got This**?
Write them below before you move onto Week Five!

WEEK FIVE

Organize, Organize, Organize

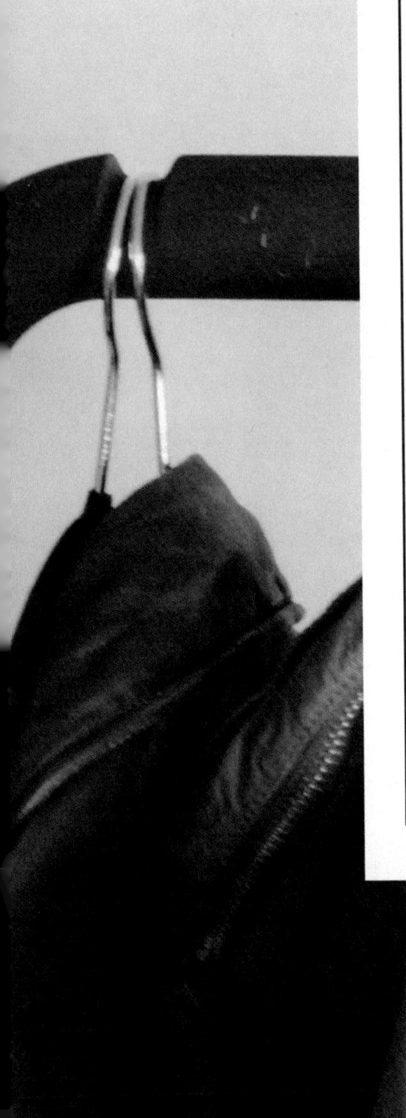

To say I'm proud of you is an understatement. You did it. You purged your closet asking yourself the right questions and you did a fabulous job. Please, please don't stop now! It can be intriguing to think, you're all done and ready to be the new you, but this is like working out and not stretching. If you don't finish properly you are gonna feel it later, and it's gonna hurt.
Now the new phase of work begins.

It's time to make sure your closet is functioning correctly for you so you can add new pieces (Week 6!) that you know you need for a fully functioning closet that makes you excited to get dressed in the morning.

This week we also talk about how to make the physical space of your closet work for you. There are so many reasons for a frustrating closet and it's not always the clothes. Sometimes it's a dark, cramped closet where items seems to hide from you. Others, in an ambitious attempt to organize, go overboard on the bins and end up making things even less organized. Tackle each section the same as you did the purge. Chunk it down and stay focused.
I believe in you!

CONFIDENCE TIP:
Your tailor should be your bestie. Having clothes that fit you will make all the difference.

Why Isn't Your Closet Working For You?

Do you find yourself stressed out every time you get dressed because you can't find your favorite sweater? Are you constantly searching for an item that you **SWEAR** you know exists but haven't been able to find it for months? Do you find that your clothes are always wrinkled because they are being squished, squeezed and rumpled in your jam-packed and chaotic closet?

I mean, can you think of anything more frustrating? This cannot be the way you start your day, girl! You have bigger fish to fry, like taking over the world, for example. So let's get down to the bottom of your closet woes to make a real, long lasting change. Below are a few suggestions on common closet frustrations. These are meant to be examples of how to tackle this assignment. Then there is space for you to get to work! It's also helpful to make a list from this exercise so you know exactly what you need to do to TAKE ACTION!

PROBLEM	SOLUTION
My closet doesn't have a lot of shelf space so I'm hanging items I'd prefer to be folded.	Purchase a canvas-shelving organizer that attaches to the closet rod at The Container Store.
My blouses always get wrinkled because they are too overcrowded in there!	Make more room in my closet by getting thinner hangers, which will help streamline the closet and allow the clothes to breathe. **- OR -** Purge any unwanted or unworn clothes. The more room, the less wrinkled they will be.
I only wear jewelry that I can see so I wear the same four pieces over and over because I don't want to go through my jewelry box every morning.	Organize my jewelry out in the open. Open shelving, cork boards etc. Time to take a trip to Target!

Problem

Solution

THE FOUR CORE PRINCIPLES FOR KILLER ORGANIZATION

When it comes to organizing your closet there are so many different things to keep in mind. Here are the four principles I've found to work in the majority of closets. That being said, this is YOUR closet. If you have found that something doesn't work for you, trust your instinct. The best way to find an organizational system that works for you is by trial and error. You may have to change your system a few times to really get it right. Following these four principles will provide clarity and understanding. That mixed with your cleared out closet and trust in your instinct will have you organized in no time!

1

SPACE:
Space is often overlooked when we are talking about closets. We like to shove, push, and squeeze our clothes into submission. I'd like to invite you to start thinking about your closet as SPACIOUS. I know!!!! Feels good, right?! It's not about filling the space because we have it, but creating a space where everything can be seen and has a wonderful, uncrowded home. Also, cramming your clothes causes wrinkles and leads to feeling overwhelmed.

2

UNIFORMITY:
Whenever you are purchasing things for your closet such as hangers, bins, and shelves, think about how to keep them uniform. It should all coordinate. Also, this keeps your closet looking pristine and like a well-oiled machine. Continue to think of the idea of uniformity as you put your clothes away as well. All your hangers should face the same way. Taking that point even further, your clothes should all go the same way on the hanger. These small acts keep your closet from falling back into a huge messy pile of clothes.

3

"KEEPING IT ALL IN THE OPEN":
When you open your closet, you want to see it ALL. Not only do you want to see it all, you should to be able to get to it easily. Now, I know that some closets are very challenging, but do your best. As long as you are keeping in mind that you actually have to be able to reach it to it to wear it, I'm sure you'll be in good shape. Keep in mind that "grab and go" is crucial and easy accessibility is *key*!

4

CATEGORIZING:
This is so important when organizing your clothes. There is a specific order I personally like to follow. To me, this is the way to make finding your clothes a breeze. That being said, I want you to ask yourself *"How do I like to get dressed in the morning and how can I implement that in my closet?"* Once again, you have been in your closet for your whole life seeing what works and doesn't work. So instead of feeling overwhelmed, allow yourself to view yourself as the expert of your own closet. Take this system as a guideline, and if something doesn't feel right to you, you can totally switch it. There is always going to be a little bit of trial by organizing fire when you implement a new system. So be open to changing as you go along.

The Kick-Ass Way To Categorize Your Clothes:

STEP ONE

TYPE

Start with identifying what category the item falls into. For example, place all your jackets together in one section of the closet. By starting here you are creating a specific place to go to when trying to locate a certain item. This will help you mix and match pieces more easily and allow you to do a rapid-fire comparison of what you've got.

STEP TWO

STYLE

After you have put all of the shirts together you can organize them by button downs, blouses, dressy t-shirts, etc. Since most women usually get dressed with a specific agenda, it makes a lot of sense to arrange it this way.

STEP THREE

COLOR

Color comes last in this process even though it's my favorite. Make sure to first organize by type and style so that you can see how many blue dresses you have. It's not as helpful to see how many blue pieces of clothing you have. You are more likely to say, *"I want to wear a blue dress today,"* than you are to say, *"I want to wear something blue."* That being said, I really do love organizing by color. It is an important step in being able to spot trends in your wardrobe. For example, I may have not realized I have a purple dress addiction if it wasn't brought to my attention by organizing my closet in this way.

BONUS STEP: SEASON

By separating your clothes by season you will be making it easier to swap out your wardrobe according to the weather. The reason this is a bonus step is because some people have houses large enough to store their off-season clothes somewhere else when they're not in use.

WAYS TO MAKE YOUR CLOSET PRETTY (AND FUNCTIONAL)

Let's face it, if a space isn't inviting, you don't want to be there. Closets aren't typically thought of as a room in your house, but if you give it some love and pay attention to the details, it'll become a room you actually love spending time in. Below are a few of my favorite easy tricks for making your closet streamlined and beautiful.

Hangers

By switching out your old hangers for uniform ones, there is an instant organized look (with very little work required)

YOUR HANGERS SHOULD BE:

- ☑ The same brand and color– When your hangers are all the same they look cleaner and take up way less space.
- ☑ Thin – I'm a big fan of thin hangers (except for suits and coats) because again, we are trying to make things look uniform and spacious.
- ☑ Not broken – Yep, I'm going there. If your hangers are broken, don't try and make it work. Throw them out. I promise, I know where you can get more.
- ☑ Appropriate for the item – If you are hanging a suit, it must be on a suit hanger. You can actually ruin a suit by keeping it on a wire hanger from the dry cleaner. Don't let that happen!

BINS: There are a ton of different styles and fabrics to choose from when getting bins for your closet. I'm not a huge fan of bins that are really large (more like hamper sized) because things just fall to the bottom, never to be seen again.

Lighting

DARK CLOSETS CAN BE THE DEATH OF A SUCCESSFUL MORNING.

Take the time to find a solution for your dark quarters.

TWO EASY FIXES: Battery Powered Mini Tap Lights AND/OR Christmas Lights

*If you have a dark closet, choose light colored shelves to make it easier to see them.

Make it Pretty

YOUR CLOSET IS A ROOM, TOO!

Making it feel special will help you to take good care of it.

- ☑ Painting the shelves or the back wall can help add a fun pop!
- ☑ Wallpaper is a fun way to make your closet unique, special, and exceptional.
- ☑ If you have a walk-in closet, a rug can really warm up the space and make it feel more personal.
- ☑ Add beautiful touches such as open shelving, bins, places for jewelry and scarves.

Key Pointers for Keeping your Clothes ON POINT

- Take the plastic off. Mildew can be trapped in the plastic. While you think you are protecting your garments, you are actually doing the opposite!

- Wire hangers ruin everything. Nothing good can come from a wire hanger. Promise.

- Keep your pants looking crisp by hanging them along their creases.

- Fold chunky sweaters so they don't get marks from the hangers.

- Don't cut the hanging loops if your dress can't stay on the hanger without it!

- Use a scarf hanger for your scarves. Without one they tend to slip or you have to tie a knot that can leave creases. They are available at specialty stores like Bed Bath and Beyond and The Container Store.

- Instead of always having your silk items dry cleaned, hand washing is actually better for the fabric.

- Wash your jeans less. If there is no pre-treatment, I advise not to wash for the first six months to ensure the jeans mold to your body. Obviously, if you get them stained this is out the window, but try your best!

- Jeans should be washed inside out in cold water.

- Cashmere sweaters should be folded in thirds to avoid the crease down the middle.

- If you have an item that you want to keep soft, use half the detergent. Then run through an extra rinse cycle. The detergent can leave a residue that leads to a less soft feel.

- Leather stretches easily, so for leather jackets put them right onto a well-formed hanger.

- Don't let your bathing suits dry in the sun. This will cause fading.

- Condition your leather boots every few months. It pays off in the end.

HOW TO CHOOSE THE *RIGHT* HAT FOR THE OCCASION

SHOES. OMG. SHOES.

Shoe organization is a huge part of your closet. Your shoes need a real home and I don't mean on the floor or in a bin. Clear open boxes, shelves, or a hanging shoe rack serve as a way to organize and declutter. A great way to save space is to place your shoes back to front. By making your shoes "spoon" like this you are saving loads of space. It's important to remember that whatever you choose, you should be able to get to them easily, see them quickly, and everything should fit without having to struggle.

THE OVER THE DOOR SHOE ORGANIZER:

This is the option for you if you have a really small closet with a door that opens (not a sliding door). You can get a few different kinds of shoe organizers for your door. I'm a fan of the one with clear pockets. That way you can see all your shoes (SO IMPORTANT) and they are less likely to fall. It really depends on the kind of shoes you own. You can also go for a wire rack or one that has little cubbies. Keep in mind your own shoes and closet situation in order to get the best solution for you.

HANGING SHOE ORGANIZER:

This is a great option for someone who has extra hanging closet space and doesn't have a lot of floor space. These hanging compartments can be great, but can sometimes get too heavy. The canvas hanging shoe bags are a great bet because they are sturdy and have deep shelves. Put lighter shoes like flip flops at the top and chunky boots at the bottom so the weight is distributed correctly.

FLOOR SHOE RACKS:

If you have space on the floor of your closet, a floor shoe rack is a great option. There are several different choices available. Again, keep in mind the specific shoes in your closet. If your shoes are relatively small, without large heels, and are compact on a shelf, you can choose a shoe cubby unit. If you find that your shoes need more space, try a more open option like a stackable shoe shelf or a shoe cabinet. Some floor shoe racks come with grips to keep shoes in place. Other great features include several different tiers, high cubbies, mesh shelves, customizable shelves, and so many more.

SHOE TREE:

Shoe trees are great for a smaller, taller space in a closet. A lot of people use shoe trees in a front hall closet or by the front door. They come in all different tiers depending on the size of your closet. A lot of shoe trees are also adjustable making them very convenient.

SHELF SHOE ORGANIZERS:

If you have a large space for your shoes, or even a separate shoe space, the ideal option is a shelf shoe organizer. One of my favorite ways to organize a large closet is with clear shoeboxes. They keep your shoes safe from dust and damage while still making them visible. A clear shoe drawer or a drop-front shoe box are nice options because they allow for easier accessibility. The key with all shoeboxes or bins is a clear aspect so you can see the shoe. Anything hidden will be forgotten.

BOOT ORGANIZATION:

Your boots usually need a separate storage system since they are tall and take up more room. It's always a plus to take good care of your boots while you store them. Boot stands, shapers, and shoe trees are all great opportunities to take care of your shoes while storing them in a smart way.

SHOE CARE: There are so many options to take care of your shoes these days that are easily accessible and easy to use. From deodorizers to shoe shines, take the time to seek out the right shoe care to make your shoes last longer and stay in better shape.

SO WHAT HAVE WE LEARNED? Week Five

- Having a spacious closet is a good thing. No need to cram, push, and shove!

- If you can't see it, you won't wear it.

- Make sure to organize by type, style, color, and season.

- Organizing your closet works best with trial and error, so you must be open to tweaking as the weeks go by.

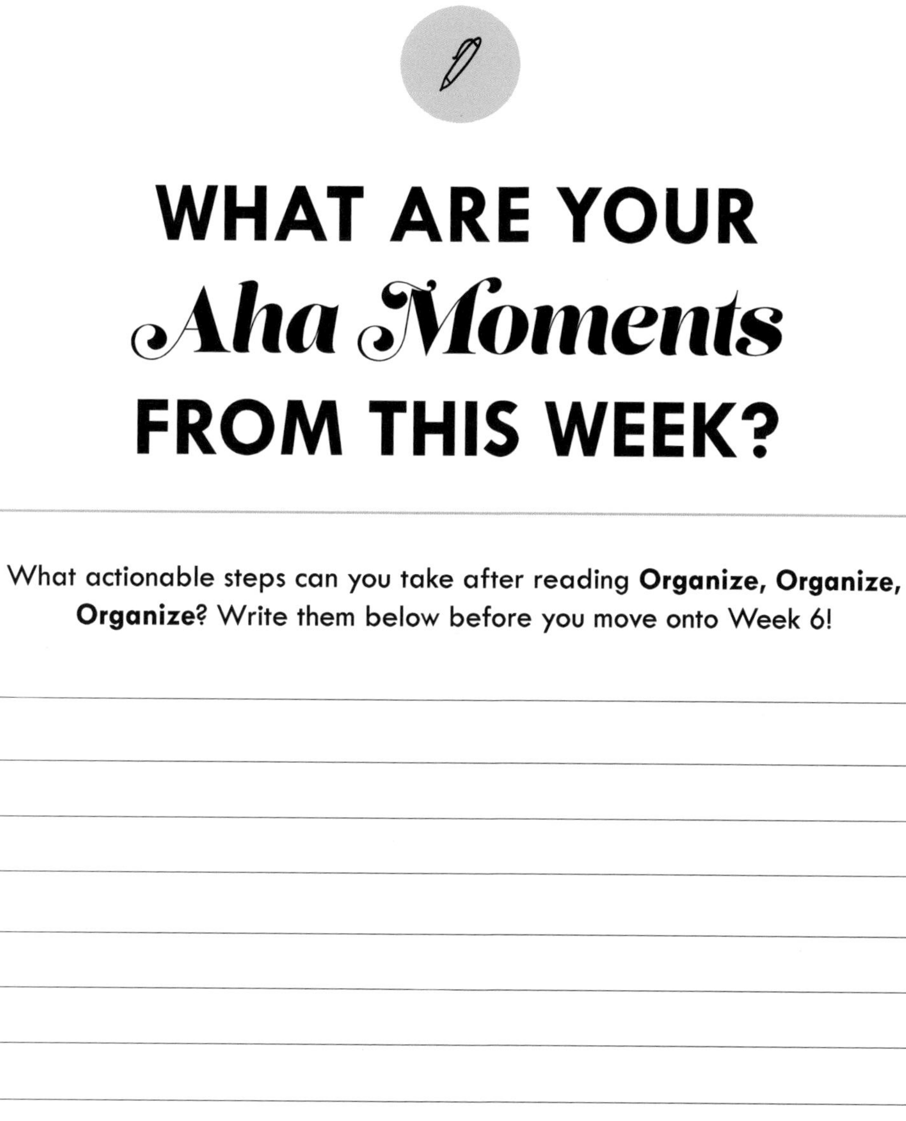

WHAT ARE YOUR *Aha Moments* FROM THIS WEEK?

What actionable steps can you take after reading **Organize, Organize, Organize**? Write them below before you move onto Week 6!

WEEK SIX

Shopping & Maintaining

There are two kinds of people. People who love shopping, and people who don't...

People who live for shopping have no idea how people can hate it, yet people who hate shopping seriously don't have any idea how anyone can think shopping is fun. Shopping is like cilantro. It's not a meh subject. It's a love or hate. Well, that is until I came along and **CHANGED YOUR MIND!**

That's right. I believe I can turn a non shopper into a shopper. Not just a shopper, a shopping lover. *How do we get there?* From minimizing possible meltdowns and maximizing the knowledge you have about yourself as you shop.

If you are someone who has a hard time shopping, make sure to not do too much in one day. There is no rule that says you have to finish buying and replacing everything you purged in one day. Actually, please don't do that. Give yourself time to find the perfect pieces that you love!

Another main culprit that causes shopping frustration is getting high hopes before getting to the dressing room. If you see a piece of clothing on a hanger that you think could be "the one," try and not get too excited. Some items have something called "hanger appeal." This means they look fabulous on a hanger but don't always work well on a body. **There is nothing wrong with trying things on and not having it work out.** Repeat that sentence please. I'll wait.

So you see, it's important to go into shopping with a fresh attitude and not take things too personal.

Shopping Online

VERSUS

Shopping in a Store

PROS OF SHOPPING *Online:*

- No lines.
- Sometimes the selection is bigger online than in the store.
- Clothes are brand new and haven't been tried on by lots of people.
- You can shop in your comfy sweats.
- You can take your time.

PROS OF SHOPPING IN A *Store:*

- Seeing the quality in person.
- No guess about whether or not it fits.
- You can ask for help.
- There is no wait - you see something and you take it home with you.
- Accessories are also available to complete the outfit.
- You can support small businesses.

ONLINE SHOPPING TIPS

1. Make sure you own a measuring tape. A lot of times stores will have a sizing chart based on measurements. *Don't guesstimate.* Knowing your measurements will ensure you get the right size.

2. Check out the model in the outfit. If the skirt is really short on her, but she's clearly 6 ft., know that the skirt will probably be longer on you if you are 5'2". A lot of sites now list the height and measurements of their models for comparison's sake.

3. Ever go online and buy something that looks COMPLETELY different once you get it in person? A lot of times clothing is clipped back or pinned on the model to make it more flattering. I know, it completely defeats the purpose of showing the fit of the garment, but it's true. When you order online, try to look for signs the shirt isn't clipped. Also have realistic expectations about what your are ordering. It will help with the disappointment of an item you have built up in your head.

4. If you can afford a dip in your bank account buy two sizes. Most sites have a free return policy as well as making it easy to return in the store. If you are unsure of your size, just buy both and return the one that doesn't fit!

IN-STORE SHOPPING TIPS

1. If you aren't sure how a garment will react to wear and tear put it through the ringer in the dressing room. It's not very nice for the sales associates but if you crumple it in a ball and it becomes a wrinkled mess that's pretty telling! Same goes for a button down that is wrinkle free. If after trying it on, it still looks like a million bucks this may be a sure fire win!

2. Find your person. If you like shopping with guidance, finding your sales associate can be KEY. There is nothing better than feeling like you have an expert in your corner. Well, besides me of course!

3. Go in with a clear vision. Shopping unfocused will lead to poor results. Go in with a list and a price point to ensure a happy ending.

The Confident Closet
FABRIC CHEAT SHEET

Knowing your fabrics can help you from making the same shopping mistakes over and over again. This list gives you the basics about fabrics so you can be confident when you shop. Always check the label, girl! Fabric is made up of fibers that are either synthetic or natural. **A natural fiber comes from an animal or plant. A synthetic fiber is man-made and usually has some plastic in it.**

NATURAL FIBERS INCLUDE:

COTTON
CASHMERE
WOOL
LINEN
ANGORA
SILK
LEATHER
HEMP

BASIC SYNTHETIC FIBERS INCLUDE:

ACRYLIC
POLYESTER
RAYON
SPANDEX
ACETATE
NYLON

If you look at a label and it says a percentage of a few different things, it means the fabric is a ***blend***. Here is an example:

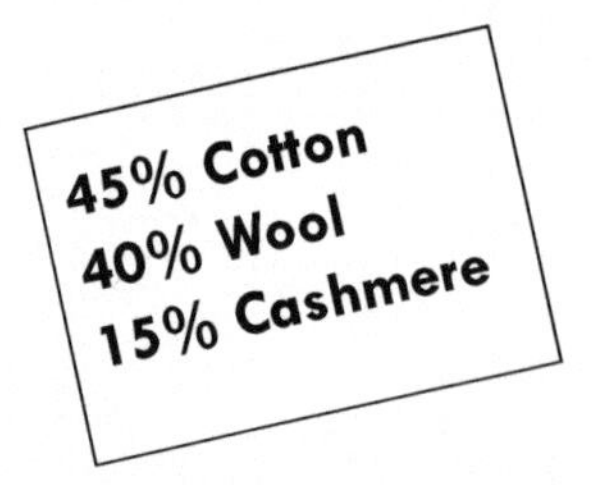

WANT TO DO THE FABRIC TEST?

If you take a small piece and hold a lighter to it, the natural fiber will smell like burning hair, and the synthetic will curl into a wax like ball. Synthetic also burns faster than natural.

SYNTHETICS are usually easy to clean and take care of. They are also less eco-friendly than natural fibers. Polyester and nylon tend to pill more easily than most natural fibers. Even if a natural fiber (such as wool) pills, they are usually easier to remove without damaging the garment. Knits with a high ratio of synthetic to natural fiber will cause your sweaters to pill more easily.

NATURAL FIBER clothing usually needs to be dry-cleaned. This is especially true about luxurious fabrics such as leather or silk. Natural fibers usually last longer than synthetic making them higher quality and usually worth the investment.

SOFT, HIGH QUALITY COTTON is great for comfort. Be careful when cleaning since it can shrink easily.

HIGH TECH SYNTHETICS are great if you are looking for active wear that breathes and absorbs moisture - this is the way to go!

IMITATION SILKS (such as rayon) are hard to clean since they get damaged in water. Also, they have a tendency to look cheap and be ill-fitting.

WHEN TO *Splurge* & WHEN TO $AVE

In the day and age where everything can be found cheaper and on sale, it's hard to know WHY we should be spending more. When does it make sense to save our money and when is it worth it to splurge a little for the sake of quality? Maybe it's the word "splurge." It feels indulgent and unnecessary when sometimes that's just not the case.

HERE ARE WAYS YOU CAN HELP RETRAIN YOUR EYE TO SPOT IF IT'S AN ITEM TO $AVE OR SPLURGE...

Splurge

• Patterns and prints are a good time to spend a little more money. Cheaper items tend to have seams that don't line up. This can be especially true with horizontal stripes!

• Good quality basics. Contrary to popular belief, I think the best time to splurge is on something you can wear over and over again.
Some examples of staples to splurge on:
- *A cashmere cardigan in a neutral color*
- *A trench coat that works for spring and fall*
- *A high quality pair of riding boots*
- *A little black dress with a perfect fit*

• A piece you LOVE that has gotten a lot of wear & tear. That is the piece that you should spend money on to replace. You know you'll wear it and you know you deserve a nicer version of it.

• Handbags are a great time to spend a little cash. Not only can a great purse elevate an entire outfit, it also will last WAY longer. Buying a purse with a cheap zipper or fake leather that peels and rips will make it more likely that you will have to buy several of them. One well made purse will last a lifetime (if you take good care of it).

• One of a kind pieces that you WILL wear. As discussed, sometimes ultra unique pieces don't get enough wear. That being said, if you find something uber special that makes you feel confident and you know no one else will have it, it seems like the PERFECT time to splurge. I mean, if you're going to splurge, splurge on something good. If you are sure you will spend your life regretting it, the answer is clear. Buy that sucker and don't look back!

$AVE

• Trendy pieces usually only last a season making them something not worth splurging on. Especially if it's a new trend that you are unsure about, it's probably not the best time to dole out the cash. Start with a cheaper version before you splurge for something you won't wear.

• A statement piece. If you aren't going to get a lot of use out of it, don't spend the money. It is essentially money hanging in your closet. As much as we love unique pieces, we get bored of them quickly because they aren't very versatile.

• Ok, now you may want to sit down for this one. Save money on jeans. While I do think there is a middle ground (not $10 and not $500) jean trends change quite often making them something you won't be wearing for years. Do you want your jeans to fit well? Absolutely. You also have to be realistic that if you wear them a ton they are going to wear out. Expensive or cheap eventually they fall apart or become dated. Also, jeans are something that are often on sale. So there are ways to find expensive jeans for a good deal. So maybe this isn't a full "save item" but more of an in between. I like to have at least three nice pairs of jeans (that I feel great in) on rotation.

• Themed outfits or costumes. So this can be an accidental splurge, but I'm calling you out! How often do you wait until the last minute for a themed party or Halloween costume? You end up spending so much money because you didn't plan ahead enough to find something affordable. Nothing makes us spend too much like desperation and the fear we have run out of time. Don't let this happen to you!

WHAT TO BRING SHOPPING

Clothing that is appropriate for the day. For example, if you are going shopping for jeans, don't wear a dress. You have to be able to see the jeans with a top that works. Also, make sure your clothes are easy to take on and off. It's can be frustrating to take your clothes on and off.

A well-fitting bra.

YOUR SHOPPING LIST! We made a master shopping list with notes back during Week 3. Make sure you have that on hand!

Any coupons!

A clean and showered version of yourself. Also helps if you are wearing makeup and you do your hair. Refer back to Week 1 if you have any questions about why this is important.

Comfy shoes. Girl, you got a big day of shopping. This ain't the time to wear stilettos.

A bottle of water or something to keep you hydrated.

Underwear that doesn't have too many lines or isn't too brightly colored. You will be surprised at how many clients I have that can't look past the fact that they can see their bright orange undies.

A snack of some kind for those last minute hunger pangs. No one wants to see you hangry. No one.

Your wallet with all the appropriate cards, cash, and IDs needed.

Your cell phone – so you can document the day and post pics on Instagram! I wanna see! #theconfidentcloset

An open mind. If you go with a negative attitude I guarantee you are going to drive yourself crazy. This is supposed to be fun!

HAPPY SHOPPING YOU INCREDIBLE "STYLE BLAZER"!

The Emotional Rollercoaster of Shopping

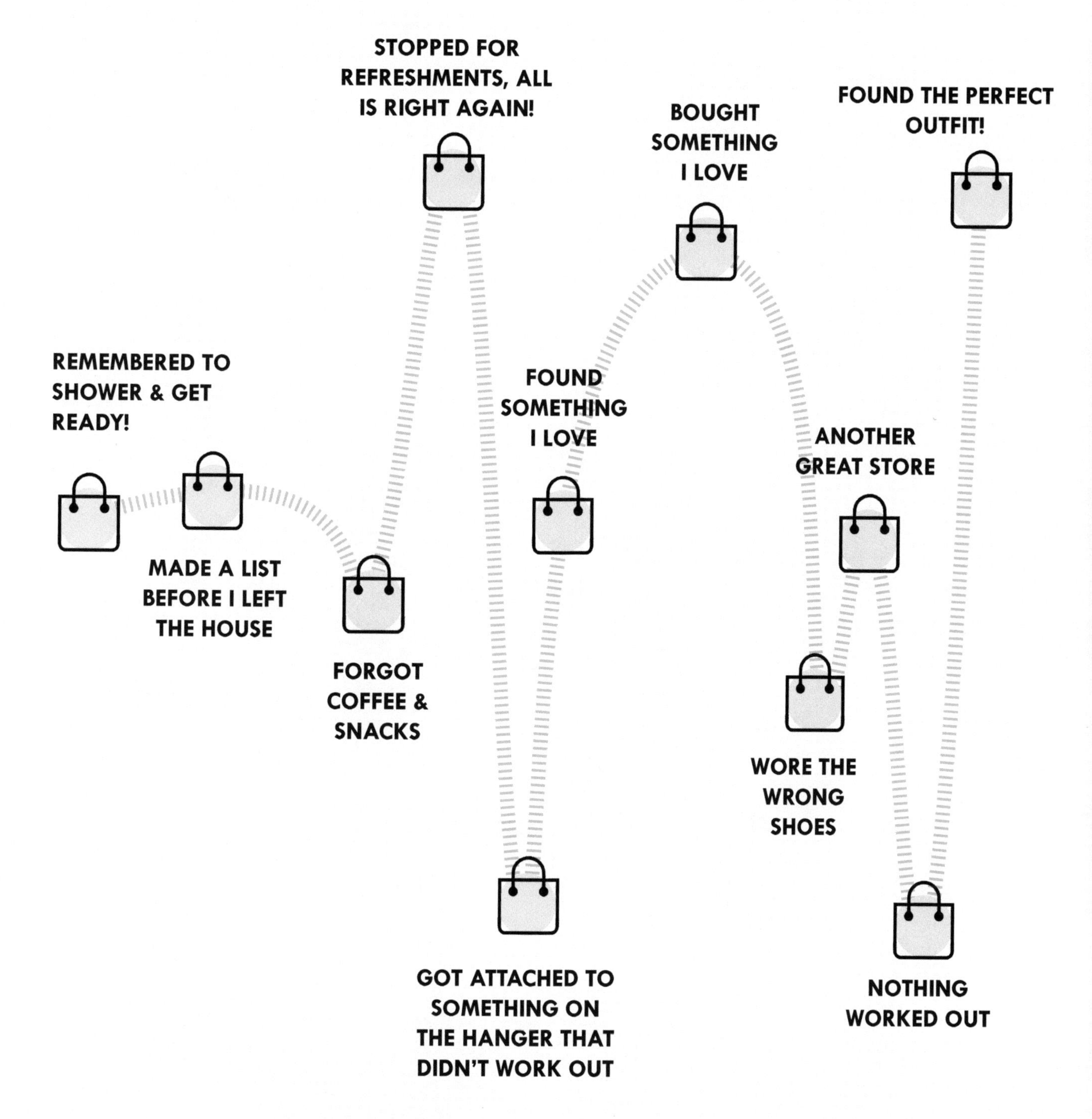

You have been shopping all day.

You started strong getting a few new fantastic dresses. You then had a stroke of bad luck at the next few stores and it put you in a slightly frustrated mood.

You started looking at your watch and begin to feel pressed for time. You decide to forget about lunch because you want to hit up a few more stores. Now that you are hungry and frustrated you start to go into stores with a bad attitude. You don't even want to try things on. You leave feeling annoyed, frustrated, and unproductive.

We have all had those days and they are THE WORST. Especially when you go with an intention to buy something specific like a dress for an event the next day. Leaving empty handed after a day of shopping really puts a damper on the day, that's for sure.

After several years of shopping WITH clients and shopping FOR clients I am now a self-proclaimed *"Efficient Enjoyable Shopping Connoisseur."* That's why I'm sharing these warning signs with you to prevent you from having another Debbie Downer shopping disaster.

TOP 3 WARNING SIGNS THAT YOU SHOULD STOP SHOPPING (AND WHAT TO DO TO HELP)

1. YOU START GETTING CRITICAL. What I find with most women is that when we first start looking through the racks we are filled with excitement and positivity. It's once we start trying on things that don't fit the way we envisioned that we start to get crabby. It's important to recognize that once you are full of negative thoughts you aren't going to like anything.

WHAT TO DO: Try to keep that positive mindset throughout your shopping experience. I do periodic check-ins with myself. Ask yourself questions such as, *"Is this rack overwhelming me? Let's check out the jewelry."* Or give yourself reminders like, *"Yes! So much cobalt blue here today! That color looks amazing on me."*

2. YOU ARE SUPER HUNGRY BUT ARE TRYING TO PUSH THROUGH. Often we go shopping as an extra errand to do. It is often around meal time (I usually shop around lunch) so sometimes we forget to eat. DON'T. You are just asking to put yourself in a funk.

WHAT TO DO: If you are hungry or thirsty you HAVE to take care of that. Nobody likes a *hangy* shopper. If this is something you find really find affects you, I suggest bringing water and snacks. It may sound silly but sometimes you gotta stop and refresh.

3. YOU BECOME GLAZED OVER AND UNFOCUSED. This means it's been too long, and it's time to take a break. Walking around in a fog is just going to make the shopping experience longer without accomplishing much. I always say I can go into a store and notice different things. That is because when you go in with a focused mind you are more efficient. This makes shopping more enjoyable and quicker as well.

WHAT TO DO: Take a break. Grab food, make a call, sit outside for a few. Afterwards you can reassess how you feel. Are you too tired to continue? Do you feel refreshed? Make the call with a clear head.

I know. I am a stylist and I am telling you to STOP shopping. This may seem counter intuitive, but when you hit a wall when you are shopping, it no longer is going to be beneficial. It can also make you leave with a bad taste in your mouth about the day. This is totally unnecessary. I want you to ENJOY shopping, feel confident in your clothes and knowledgeable in the stores. So next time you are out and start to see one of these warning signs, I want you to check in and reassess.

CHANGING OLD HABITS

What habits do you feel have been causing you harm when it comes to your clothes? After going through your closet so thoroughly, you should have found some patterns. Maybe it's that you buy clothes that you THINK you are going to like, but since you don't think it looks flattering it still has the tags on it. Another example could be that you find something on sale and you buy it thinking, *"I'll alter this,"* or *"It's not my style, but it's such a good deal!"*. On the next page is a place to write each bad habit. Take the time to write it down. Then write down how you can change this. Continue to refer back to this. Every time you are thinking about buying something I want you to take a second and consider,

"Am I **REPEATING** *my bad habit? Or* **CORRECTING** *it?"*

Habit	Correction

Let's Talk About *Maintenance*

You have come SO far and should be so proud of yourself. Not only are you looking fabulous but your closet is organized and filled with clothes you love. So before you feel like the work is done, let's talk about how you are going to keep it like that!

PERIODIC CHECK-INS ARE A MUST.

There are inevitably going to be those times when you start to slip into old habits. Make sure you are continually asking yourself the same questions you did during your initial purge.

Over time the clothes that you love right now will become worn or won't fit you the way they do right now. I know, it's sad but it's unavoidable. So make sure you are constantly reevaluating and saying goodbye to the clothes that you aren't wearing or that you've worn to the point of no return. Hopefully, there will be items that stand the test of time and that are classic lifelong pieces, but don't expect every piece to be that for you. It won't be that way, and that's OK. Just make the change!

If you are a sucker for an item of clothing with a story or memory, then you are really going to have to check in with your closet (and yourself) every few months. Make sure you are only keeping and wearing clothes you truly love NOW.
Dry cleaning, ironing, and steaming will all make you stand out and take your look to the next level.

Have fun and play in your closet. Make outfits at night so you have time to create unexpected looks. This will keep things fresh and exciting.

This book is ALWAYS here and so am I.
This is a journey but we are in it together.
TRUST THE PROCESS AND TRUST YOURSELF!

SO WHAT HAVE WE LEARNED?
Week Six

- You can learn to love shopping. It's all about setting yourself up for success.

- Splurge on basics and save on trendier pieces.

- When shopping, look for the warning signs before you crash.

- There are pros and cons to shopping in a store vs. shopping online. Know what works for you!

WHAT ARE YOUR *Aha Moments* FROM THIS WEEK?

What actionable steps can you take after reading **Shopping and Maintaining**?

YOU MADE IT!

Now for the moment of truth...

Are you going to do all this work just to end up in the same place in a few months? I hope not, so let's chat.

It's important to know that maintaining your closet will always be a part of having the closet you want. The exciting part is that you already know the questions to ask and have done the BIG closet clean out. So now it's an easier job. The occasional check in is usually all you need to keep your closet on track. Maybe you realize a dress you thought you'd wear has sat in your closet for the last year. You now have the tools to ask yourself the right questions quickly and effortlessly. You now know where to bring the dress to donate or give it to a friend. You also know if it's time to replace it or if you have something similar that you wear more instead. All this knowledge is life-altering, but it's up to you to stick with it and not allow yourself to fall into the same bad habits. If you find yourself starting to allow your closet to get cluttered or unorganized, take the time to ask yourself what's not working. Trust your instincts!

You also may find that the organizational system you put into place needs some tweaking. Don't get frustrated - just take the time to make the changes swiftly. There is a trial and error to figuring out the perfect system for your closet and the way you think when you are getting ready. Think of every challenge as an opportunity to getting closer to your ultimate closet! By doing the deep work you did over the last six weeks, I hope you truly feel that sense of accomplishment and ease that we discussed in the beginning of this book. Remember this feeling! It'll keep you inspired to keep it up and not fall back into bad habits. I believe in you and trust that you can believe in yourself! Confidence isn't born overnight. It comes with truly knowing who you are and showing up for yourself daily. We are all on this journey together, and **I can't wait to see where your new found confidence will take you.**

For more style tips, tricks for organizing like a pro, and ways to feel like the most confident version of yourself, check out all that Melanie has to offer:

THECONFIDENTCLOSET.COM

Instagram: *@melaniekluger*

Pinterest: *pinterest.com/theconfidentcloset*

Request to join the private Facebook group
'Real Conversations About Style With Melanie'

Contributors:

AUTHOR

MELANIE KLUGER

DESIGN & LAYOUT

JILLIAN SANDREY

PHOTOGRAPHY

ROSA DELGADO

EDITOR

COLIN KENNEDY

CONTRIBUTING EDITOR

DANI KIM

SELECT HAIR + MAKEUP

ELEVATIONS

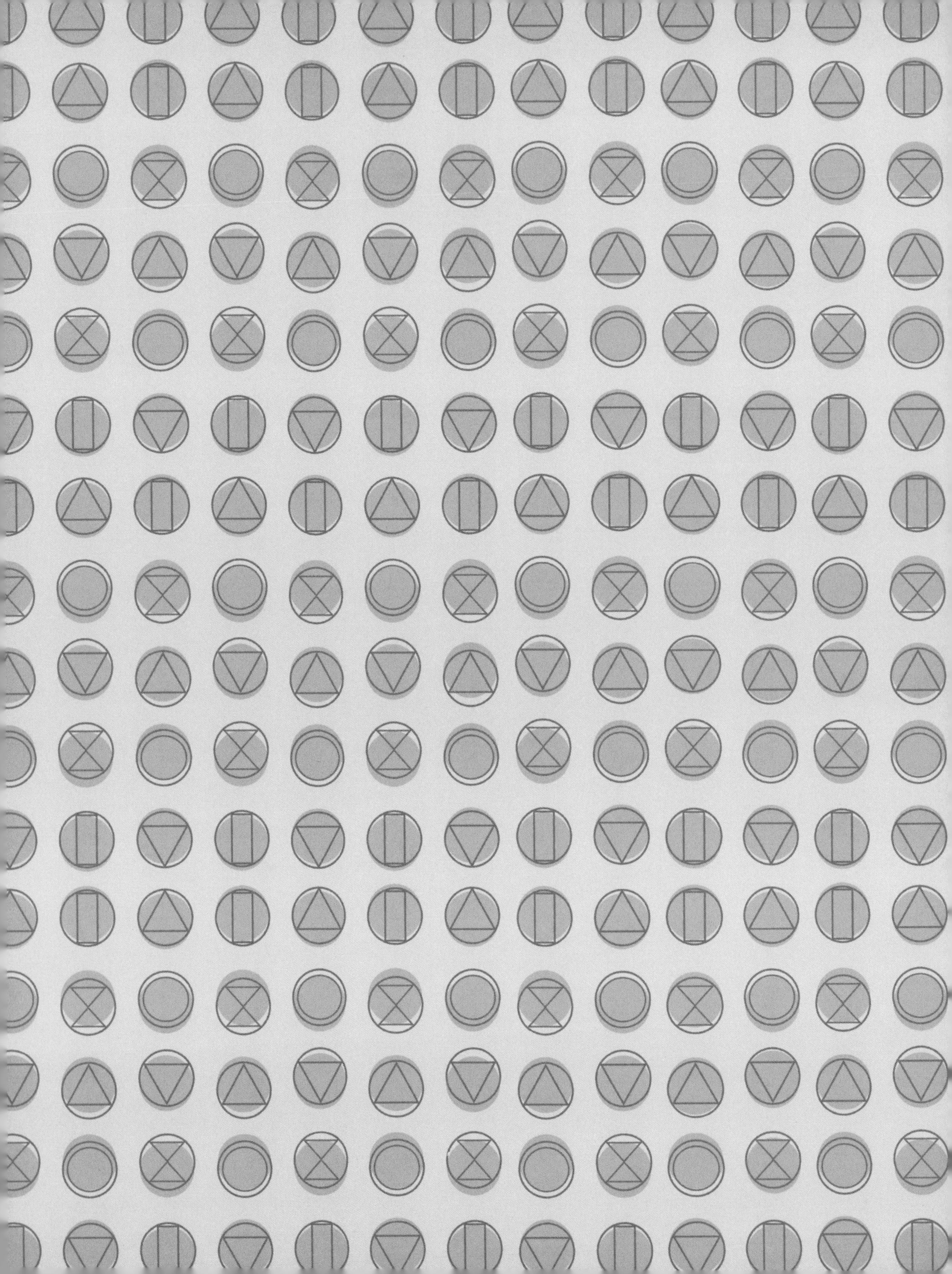

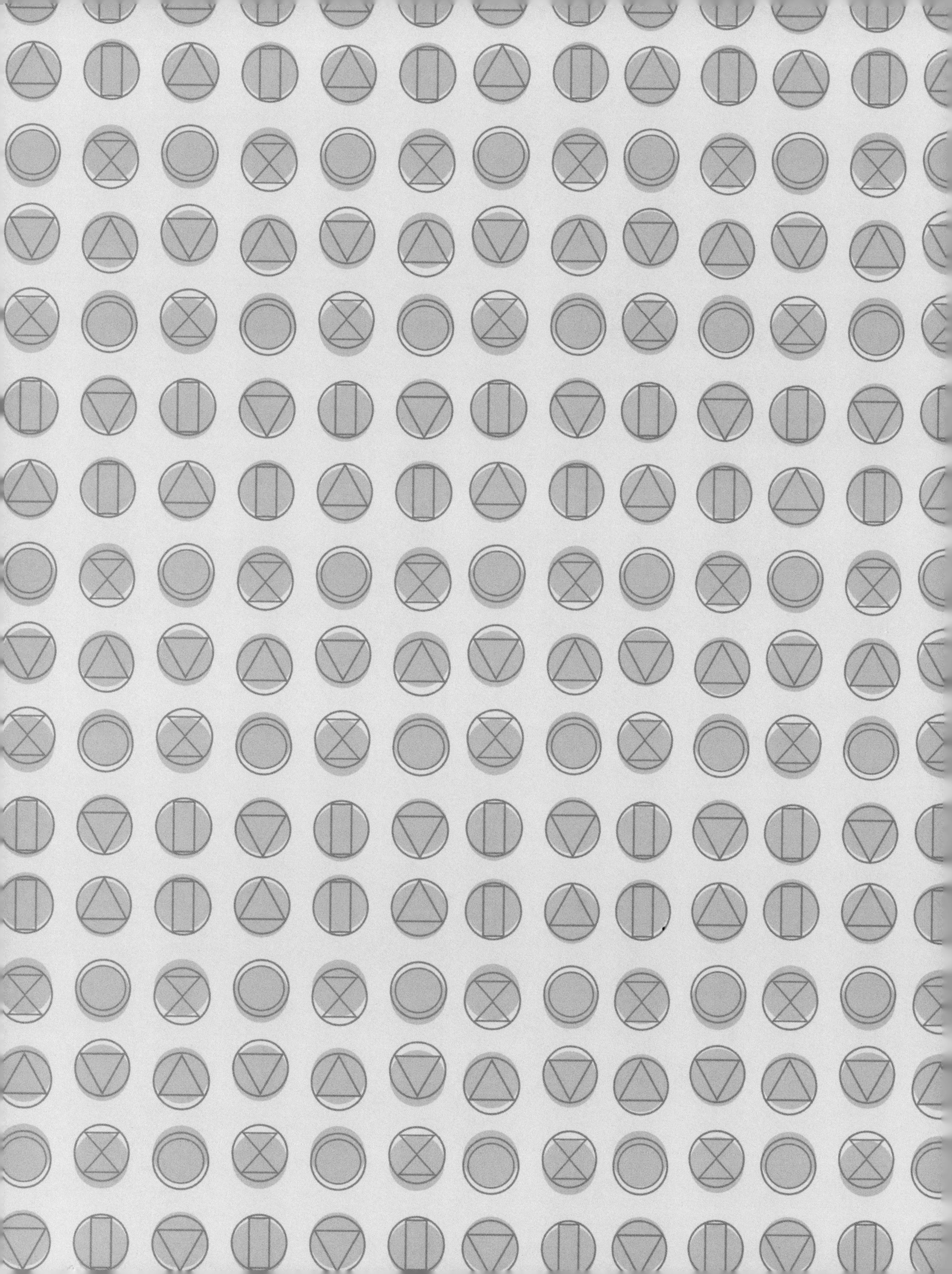

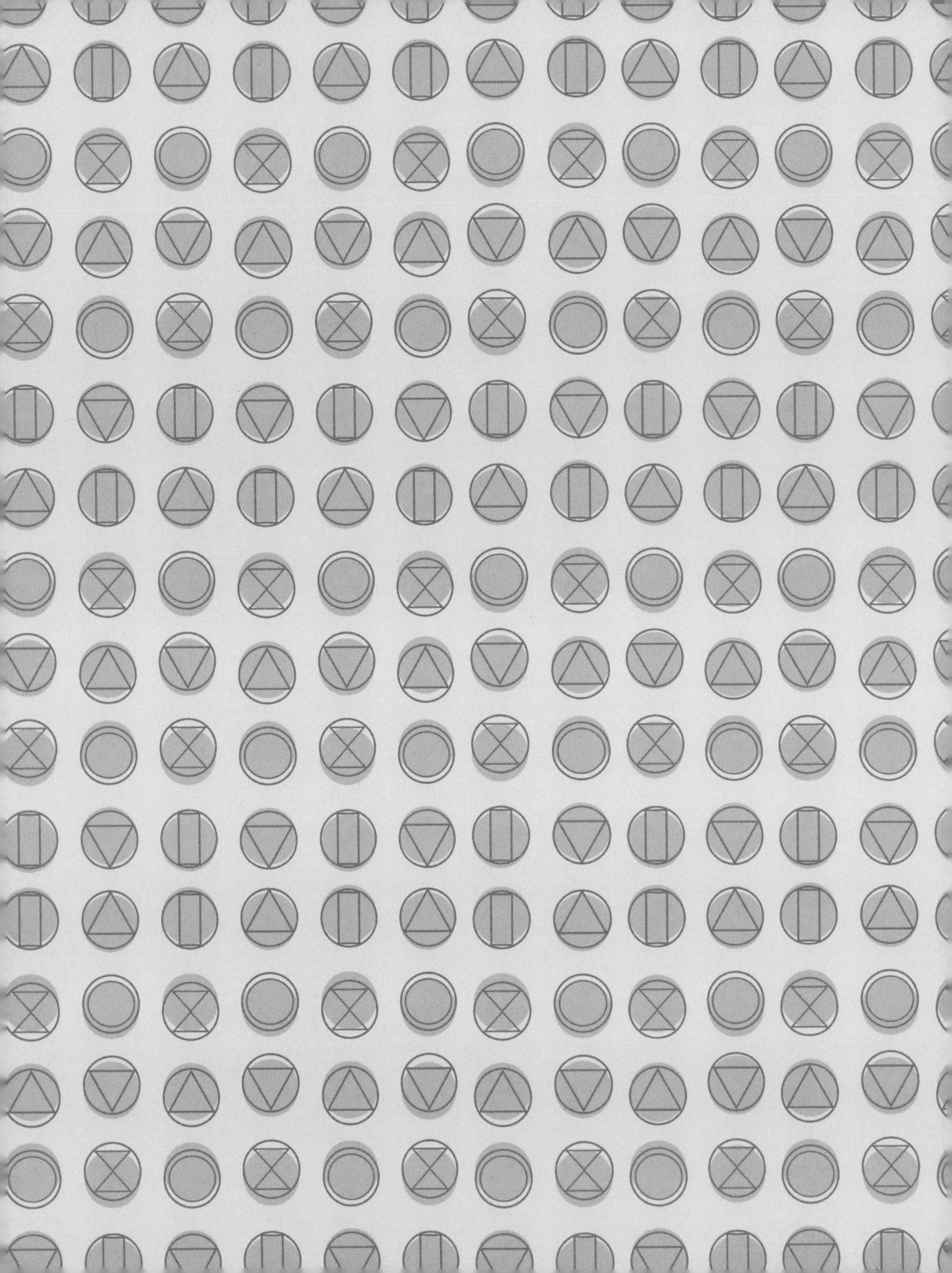

CPSIA information can be obtained at www.ICGtesting.com
Printed in the USA
BVIW12n1312200918
527977BV00009B/48